Without the Miracle There Is Nothing!

Devotionals to Encourage and Inspire

by Geoffrey Butcher

ISBN-13: 978-1496001993
ISBN-10: 1496001990

These devotionals appeared in the *News-Democrat & Leader*,
Russellville, Kentucky, between 2011 and 2013. Reproduced
by permission.

Edited by Deborah W. Butcher
Cover image from Trinity Episcopal Church,
Russellville, Kentucky.

CONTENTS

ABOUT THE AUTHOR

The Rev. Geoffrey Butcher is currently Priest-in-Charge of Trinity Episcopal Church in Russellville, KY. He came to Trinity Church after serving at Christ Church Cathedral, Nashville, where he was Canon Pastor. Prior to that he was Canon Precentor and Sub-Dean at The Cathedral Church of St. John, Albuquerque, New Mexico. Earlier in his ministry, he served as a parish priest, pastor, and organist-choirmaster for churches in New Mexico.

In addition to his primary roles as pastor, priest, and teacher, he has been a leader at numerous liturgical and church music conferences, and is active in leading centering prayer workshops and retreats. Centering prayer is a method of contemplative prayer or Christian meditation, placing a strong emphasis on interior silence.

Geoffrey was ordained a deacon in 1965 and priest in 1966 and holds a Doctorate in Ministry (parish revitalization) degree from McCormick Theological Seminary, Chicago, Illinois; a Master of Arts degree from New Mexico Highlands University, Las Vegas, New Mexico; and a Master of Divinity from The General Theological Seminary, New York City. He received his undergraduate degree from Hobart College, Geneva, New York.

From 1980-1986, he was a member of the Episcopal Church's Standing Commission on Church Music, which was responsible for the production of the Hymnal 1982. He has written numerous short sacred musical works, most notably the Rio Grande Mass.

INTRODUCTION

The devotionals in this book first appeared in the *News-Democrat* & *Leader* in Logan County, Kentucky. Each Friday a devotional is included on the religion page. I enquired if I might write some of these and was encouraged to do so by the Managing Editor, Chris Cooper. Having contributed for several years, I mentioned to Deborah Butcher, a family member, that it might be fun to have some of my devotionals printed in a little book. As a professional editor, she surprised me by taking my whim seriously and has prepared this book for your edification. Without her help this venture would never have been accomplished.

While I claim no expertise as an original thinker I enjoy retelling the story of God's presence in human life. Much of what we know comes from the scriptures, but the story is not just about people of the past. God's DNA is within each of us, just as it was within prophets and apostles. The story is about us as well as them. The goal is to live our own stories as we venture to discover the great Mystery alive in the present moment.

These devotionals tell some of those stories as experienced through my life. I have often quoted writers that I admire so that you might benefit from their insights as well. Of primary importance is to read the devotionals while reflecting on your own spiritual journey. Perhaps a thought or phrase may awaken a reality within you that you wish to uncover. Your love affair with God is the most important part. May that relationship grow and flourish.

Without the Miracle There Is Nothing!

"And what is that miracle?" you might ask.

Take the miracle of creation:

The earth we walk on – the air we breathe – the water we drink and the seeds we plant – stars and galaxies – tiny birds and creeping creatures. All had a source, and not one did we create. Was it by accident or by design?

Take the miracle of yourself – Alive:

- to know that you can think, and by ingenuity and action shape your history and that of others;
- to know that it makes a difference what you do with what you've got; to touch, see and smell – to love and hate – to cry and sing.

Take still another miracle – the miracle of finding something within you that is also outside of you. How can you sit in your room and think, or kneel before the altar and pray – and, by yourself, not be alone?

A still small voice within seems to speak and tells you of things beyond yourself. While in the present you understand that your history began before you were born, and that your future is in hands too big to fill.

We are products of a miracle; and without that miracle there is nothing.

Imagine this nothingness:

As you lie on your bed in the dark of night, imagine what it would be "not to be." Think of the energies of your day – the things you did to stay alive – the things you did to make your time worthwhile; the things you did to shape your future. What would the absence of these things mean? Then pinch yourself to know that you're still alive; but remember – in nothingness the pinch would not be felt.

Being and nothingness, the tools and alternatives of philosophers and theologians, is the colossal question which makes the whole experience of life important or unimportant.

Some thinkers have been so baffled by the miracle of existence that in order to control it they disclaim it. Philosophers like Schopenhauer (1788-1860) and Sartre (1905-1980) claim that the world is man's idea and dismiss the initial source of creation as mere "givenness" – yet, they rely on the laws of nature to describe life's events; and by claiming only limited vision, lived their lives in perpetual pessimism. Numerous agnostics and atheists have perpetuated this view, claiming only those things that can be explained rather than claiming the miracle.

Christians are different. Christians are not afraid of the miracle. We claim it and we name it.

Creation, the most obvious of our perceptions, is proclaimed, not ignored. The source of all that is deserves a name, and a name greater than any other – a name that can describe the indescribable.

We call the miracle God – the creator of all that is, and who enables us to be co-creators as well. Instead of discrediting the obvious, we worship the Source.

Christians welcome the opportunity to ask questions about themselves; and whereas none of us chose to be born, we choose to take ourselves seriously – and in so doing, discover another miracle.

We find a miracle in Bethlehem, and become wise as the Magi who discovered that manger. We find the unexplainable made simple – the immensity of God made specific. We find God in the person of Jesus. And this Jesus teaches us what to do with what we have. We accept what is and make it grow. And the food for this growth is love, in and through and around each other, which tells us what God wants us to know – that God is Love. And with this love, there is joy.

Christians claim another miracle – that we are not alone. We find a Spirit within us – yet beyond us, that gives meaning and purpose to the present and which carries us into the future. This miracle has a name too. It is a name used to describe the awesomeness, beauty and hope that we are given to feel. We call the miracle the Holy Spirit. And there is peace.

Remember the Miracle when you try to make sense out of life – and claim it. By claiming the miracle you know where you came from. By claiming the miracle you can discover meaning for your life. By claiming the miracle you can glance into your future and see where you are going. Claim nothing for your life, and that's what you'll get – nothing. But by living the miracle you will find that it is true.

Which do you choose?

Holding the Lamb

The imagery of Jesus as the Good Shepherd is one of the most familiar metaphors in Scripture. Even from the Old Testament we understand our relationship to God to be that of sheep in the loving care of a good shepherd. "The Lord is my shepherd; I shall not want. He makes me to lie down in green pastures; he leads me beside the still waters." (Psalm 23:1-2)

Although it is likely that the shepherd imagery used in the twenty-third psalm and in John's Gospel relates more to royal imagery with the Lord being a ruler, it still evokes an idealized uncomplicated country life as portrayed in pastoral poetry. In either case, there is the sense that one should place oneself under the direction of the Lord who is the touchstone of truth.

The shepherd's care for his sheep is a frequent theme in the other Gospels as well. The shepherd protects his sheep from wolves, knows his sheep by name, and seeks those that are lost. In one parable the Good Shepherd is quite ready to leave ninety-nine perfectly well-behaved sheep in the wilderness to look for, as Desmond Tutu writes, "not an attractive, fluffy little lamb – fluffy little lambs do not usually stray from their mummies – but for the troublesome, obstreperous old ram. This was the one on which the Good Shepherd expended so much energy."

We think of God as our shepherd, of Jesus as the Good Shepherd, and often of clergy as shepherds within the household of faith. Every Christian, in fact, is called to be a shepherd, a minister by virtue of baptism. Every Christian is commissioned to proclaim Christ's resurrection and to seek and serve Christ in all persons.

Artists often picture Jesus as the Good Shepherd holding a lamb. We understand that each one of us is a lamb that Jesus holds. And if we too are meant to be shepherds, there are those we need to hold as well. Love moves us into that caring ministry to one another. And when Grace surrounds us we become the hands and heart of God to the sick, the lonely, and those in need, to the lost and obstreperous, to the fluffy lamb and to those who are battered rams.

In my office I have a picture of St. Joseph holding Jesus. In a bedroom in my home I have two pictures of Mary holding Jesus. And when I think about Jesus as the Good Shepherd, I sometimes think about reversing the roles. Instead of Jesus holding me, what would it be like to hold Jesus just as Mary and Joseph held their son? I can't hold on to the thought very long, because if the thought became a reality it would be too overwhelming to bear. I doubt that I could live up to the responsibility of holding him or be sure enough of myself to accept the privilege.

If by some miracle we were able to hold Christ, how would that affect the way we live our lives? Would we want Jesus to hear and see some of the things we say or do? Would we want to put Jesus back in his car seat so we could continue our road or interior rage? Would we turn his eyes away from an orphan child who has no one to hold her? Could we risk letting him leave our hands, as Mary did, and then find him again in our arms at the foot of the cross? Would we dare risk our lives for the sake of love?

While it is an intimidating thought to hold the Lamb of God, the Christ, it is a privilege and responsibility given to us. Christ's Spirit dwells within each of us and we are called to love that Christ even, as Mother Theresa put it, in his "distressing disguise." The reversal of roles is a gift God gives us to share in Love's redeeming work.

Perhaps in our prayers we should think about holding the Christ. How would that affect our own gentleness and generosity? How would that endearing relationship move our hearts to compassion for others? Is the privilege of holding the Lamb of God too beautiful to bear?

Looking at the Bible

The Bible is central to Christian belief and practice. The Holy Scriptures show God at work in nature and history and set forth the life and teachings of Jesus. For believers they are the Word of God, trusting that God inspired their human authors and that God still speaks to us through the Bible. To receive the message, some pray that we may "hear the Scriptures, read, mark, learn, and inwardly digest them." This reflects a desire to understand God's relationship to us and to embrace the new life of love found in Christ.

In this practice there are various ways one can look at the Bible. There are questions to ask such as, "How did we get the Bible? What is its authority for our lives? How shall we interpret it?" We might also wonder why so many sacred writings were left out of the Bible.

In our study we discover that believing Christians are divided on the way the Bible should be interpreted and received. On one side of the divide are fundamentalists and many conservative evangelical Christians who typically see the Bible as the inerrant and infallible Word of God. On the other side are moderate-to-liberal Christians, mostly in mainline denominations, who continue to research the origins of these texts, have guidelines for applying their authority, and who are open to interpretations that speak to present day culture. They recognize that the Bible was written in ancient times and addressed to people of that day. It is an artifact of this world, the work of human minds and lips and hands, under the inspiration of their experience with God. Just as we make errors trying to determine the mind of God, so should the scribes' assumptions be revisited in the light of present day experience and the inspiration of the Holy Spirit. For many an appropriate approach to the Bible is to view it as "faith preaching to faith," that is, the story of people in relationship to God and to one another telling their stories over and over again as they journey in faith. It is the story of people searching for God and of God's search for us. It is the story of creation and recreation, of calling and restoration, of blessing and forgiveness, of empowering leaders, kings, prophets, until ultimately God comes in Jesus Christ. Clearly, the major theme that runs throughout the Bible from Genesis to Revelation is God's ceaseless search for humanity.

The Bible is a library of books containing a variety of types of literature. There is myth, as in the creation stories found in the Book of Genesis. There is history, with records of the life of the Jewish people, of Jesus, and of early Christians. There are ancient hymns as found in the Psalms. There is speculation too regarding the end of time and the final coming of the Kingdom of God. There are exhortations to repent and compassionate words of healing. There are stories of humanity's unfaithfulness to God and words conveying the love and mercy of God to restore all things to the Godhead.

If we pray that we may "hear, read, mark, learn, and inwardly digest" the Scriptures, we need to proceed from an informed point of view. It is not good enough to assume that this study is as simple as a contemporary bumper sticker boldly puts it, "God said it, I believe it, and that settles it." Nor can we be satisfied to rely on what some call "the old-time religion" which is as new as nineteenth and twentieth century Protestant theology. Interpreting the Bible literally from beginning to end, unless the language of a particular passage is clearly metaphorical, is a modern practice not typical of previous centuries of Biblical inquiry. We have to approach our study from a humble stance, recognizing that the purpose of the study is not to get it right so as to club others into belief, but to participate in a living story of God's revelation to us now.

The revelation of God did not stop with the library of books we call the Bible. The story continues to be told and to develop. The Scriptures in themselves show a continuing revelation from the concept of many Gods to one God, and to a God most clearly seen in the person of Jesus Christ. It is a current revelation to help us discover who we are, what our identity is, and what it means to be a child of God. Each generation must discover anew the God that dwells within each person.

The Word of God that we truly seek to understand is not limited to the words contained in the Bible. That would be idolatrous. Our faith is not in a book but in a living relationship with our Creator, Redeemer, and Giver of Life. The Word we seek to understand, as the Gospel of John puts it, is the Word that "became flesh and lived among us." (John 1:14) It is a relationship with the God above and the God within that we are meant to discover. It is for that purpose that we receive the Biblical story and tell it over and over again, making that story of love and new life our own, and living it out together in community.

Jesus Loves Me (But He Can't Stand You)

A friend shared a song with me by Don Peters called,
"Jesus Loves Me (But He Can't Stand You)."
The text goes like this:
I know you smoke, I know you drink that brew
I just can't abide a sinner like you
God can't either, that's why I know it to be true
That Jesus loves me, but he can't stand you
I'm going to heaven, boys, when I die
Cause I've crossed every "t" and I've dotted every "i"
My preacher tells me that I'm God's kind of guy;
That's why Jesus loves me, but you're gonna fry.
God loves all his children, by gum

7

That don't mean he won't incinerate some
Can't you feel those hot flames licking you
Woo woo woo.
I'm raising my kids in a righteous way
So don't be sending your kids over to my house to play
Yours will grow up stoned, left-leaning, and gay;
I know Jesus told me on the phone today.
Jesus loves me, this I know
And he told me where you're gonna go
There's lots of room for your kind down below
Whoa whoa whoa.
Jesus loves me but he can't stand you
  (Lizard Vision FF 70569; No Moo Music/BMI)

This song is a parody, of course, on that favorite old Sunday school hymn, "Jesus loves me, this I know, for the Bible tells me so." But we also realize that this song, even as a spoof, reflects the attitude of some people.

I remember as a child attending a parochial school that taught that if you were not a member of that denomination you would go to hell. Classmates who liked me kept trying to persuade me to join the church. My solution was to ask my parents to send me to a different school.

My experience isn't unique. A variety of religious and secular organizations determine who the good guys are and who are the bad guys – who's in and who's out. Often the standard is determined by delineating prejudices. Racial and ethnic preferences often set the stage for those that "Jesus loves" and those who deserve to "fry."

I remember in the fifties speaking with a seminary professor who explained that black people do not have souls in the same sense that white people do. Salvation for blacks was questioned in his mind. Today we hear of a variety of groups organized to purge a nation or the world of undesirable people. The ethnic cleansing in Bosnia was a reminder of the Nazi atrocities against Jews, Russians, Poles and others. Racial, ethnic, religious and political cleansings are rampant in multiple countries. And one doesn't need to look far to realize that the words of a funny song are often believed: "Jesus loves me, but he can't stand you."

We would like to think that there is but one Gospel – a Gospel of good news that mutual respect is meant to be shared among all people; and that for Christians, Jesus loves not only me, but you, whoever you may be. But we know that even within the Christian Church the Gospel is interpreted and proclaimed in so many ways, some of which are not good news.

Turmoil has been going on in the Church since the days of St. Paul. People have been trying to "get it right," and whatever theological position holds power can subdue the opponents with witch hunts, book burnings, and executions. This is our tragic history, and each generation struggles with the issue of God's acceptance of them and their acceptance of one another.

For us the question remains, does Jesus love me and does he love you? Is new life with God an option for all of us? Did God show love for the people of this world in a limited fashion or is the opportunity for a loving relationship with God available for all?

The Johannine Community, reflecting on Jesus' relationship with his heavenly Father, wrote that "God so loved the world that he gave his only Son, so that everyone who believes in him may not perish but may have eternal life. Indeed, God did not send the Son into the world to condemn the world, but in order that the world might be saved through him." (John 3:16-17)

A friend of mine, L. William Countryman, who is a Biblical scholar, expresses this truth when he writes that "creation is beloved of the creator. However much (creation) may have become estranged, it is not God's objective to take vengeance on it; rather to call it back into that right relationship, which is true and everlasting life."

"To be deprived of God is to be deprived of our own existence. Yet, the estrangement is real and is not to be overcome by divine fiat. The sending of the Son does not force salvation on anyone, but makes it possible for those who, for whatever mysterious reasons, are or become doers of the truth."

We struggle with light and darkness, with good and evil. When we see corruption in the world we rise up in horror and are prone to condemn the perpetrators. But our own darkness may stifle a generous spirit; and if we are not careful, our outlook on others can display condemnation rather than compassion. It is the darkness of our souls that motivates condemnation of others. If we could stay in the light, our motive would be to bring hope where there is despair; joy where there is sadness; pardon where there is injury; union where there is discord; and as St. Francis again prays, "love where there is hatred." (A Prayer attributed to St. Francis)

The incarnation of Love into human life was a demonstration of God's compassion for us and God's willingness to share in our struggle with light and darkness, with good and evil. This focus of eternal love into life was initiated not to condemn us, but to give us a new birth of the Spirit. This gift is not forced on us, and many may not choose to accept it. But whether or not one accepts the gift, love remains faithful: "Jesus loves me and he loves you too."

Rich toward God

The story Jesus told about the rich man who tore down his barns to built bigger ones may make us feel uneasy. (Luke 12:13-21) The story, of course, has nothing to do with farming, and it makes sense that if you have a good harvest, new barns may be in order. Jesus' point was that life does not consist in the abundance of possessions – of which many of us are greatly blessed. The presenting question is: do we rely on those possessions as the source of our happiness? Are we like the rich man who said to himself, "Soul, you have ample goods laid up for many years; relax, eat, drink, be merry." But the story concludes by God saying to him, "You fool! This very night your life is being demanded of you. And the things you have prepared, whose will they be?" So it is, Jesus said, "with those who store up treasures for themselves but are not rich toward God."

Recent studies regarding happiness have shown that great wealth doesn't necessarily make one happier – in fact, people with fewer goods seem to be happier in general. There are practical problems with owning too much – insurance, multiple bills, upkeep, security, etc. I knew one family, for example, who seldom took trips because someone had to be home to protect the property from vandals. Their castle became a prison. But perhaps the biggest problem with possessions comes when our identity depends on what we own, what we do, what we know, and what other people think of us. Am I what I do, what I know, what I control? The energy to maintain that kind of identity often leaves little room to nurture a relationship with God. Eventually we will give up all that we own; and when that time comes, who will we be?

The spiritual journey is filled with paradoxes. One of them is that while God is often seen in things, as in creation, God is also profoundly known in nothingness. When we cease to put our trust in things and empty ourselves, the resulting vacuum gives God the opportunity to fill us with the gifts and fruits of the Spirit.

A story is told from the Hindu tradition that sheds light on this dilemma. A very wise and holy man wanted nothing more than that his son gain a deep knowledge of the Hindu scriptures – the Vedas – and then learn to move beyond their mere words into their essence. So when the time was ripe he sent his son to study and serve with another wise teacher.

After many years of intense study the son returned home. One afternoon the father asked, "My dear son, tell me what you have learned so far."

"Oh, Father," his son replied with outstretched palms and puffed up chest, "Not only have I learned everything that knowledge can possibly teach, but I have also mastered the arts, the sciences, and philosophies."

"Is that so, my son?" his father replied. "Then tell me! Have you sought that knowledge through which the unheard becomes heard, the un-thought becomes thought, and the unknown becomes known?"

Listening to that single question, the son realized the severe limitations of his acquired knowledge and humbly asked his father for further instructions.

The next day his father took his son to various shops in the city, including a pottery shop with many different vessels for sale. He showed his son that all the different vessels, no matter what shape, size, or name, came from a lump of clay. He did the same in a goldsmith shop – showing his son that all things there had originated from a lump of gold. Iron things, he showed him, came from a lump of iron.

As he took his son home, the father repeated their discovery and concluded one should seek that Reality, that essence, which pervades the whole of the universe.

When he saw how eager his son now was to hear about this Reality, he asked him to pick a large piece of fruit from a nyagrodha tree. He told him to break the fruit open and tell him what was within. "There are many seeds within," the son replied. His father then asked him to break open the seed. "What is within?" asked the father. The son looked into the seed and discovered that there was nothing inside.

"Nothing?" his father asked.

"Yes, nothing," the son replied.

"Hmm! There is nothing inside the seed!" repeated the father. "Yet, it is from this nothingness that this mighty tree has come into being. So you see it is this very nothingness, this invisible and subtle essence, which pervades the whole universe. You are that my son! And that is the Reality." (*In the Stillness You Will Know*, pp. 105-107)

Contemplatives in all religions have discovered that Reality, spelled with a capital 'R,' is often found in nothingness – in emptiness. As in a clay vessel, it is the space within that makes it useful. As Lao Tsu said, "Cut doors and windows for a room; it is the holes which make it useful.

Thirty spokes share the wheel's hub; it is the center hole that makes it useful. Therefore profit comes from what is there; usefulness from what is not there."

In the spiritual journey it is often what is not there that is most useful; for in the place of nothingness God's presence is most deeply felt. A glimpse of that Reality requires that we let go of our attachments; and with a humble heart enter into the stillness – into a place of nothingness, where God can fill our empty vessels with gifts of love, joy, and peace.

Is Tomorrow Judgment Day?!

(First published May 20, 2011)

Harold Camping of Family Radio has predicted that May 21, 2011, is Judgment Day. This will be the first Day of Judgment when 200 million people will be saved with the remainder perishing to damnation. October 21, 2011, will be the end of the world. Publicity of this event has been seen on 1,200 billboards nationwide and 2,000 more in dozens of foreign countries. Family Radio is broadcast on 150 radio stations. Evidence for the Rapture on this date is allegedly provided by Biblical citations found in the Book of Daniel, the Revelation to John, the First and Second Letters of Peter, and other passages.

According to Camping the Holy Spirit has not been active in any church since 1988. This is a sign that the end is near. Since then Satan has been ruling the Church and the world. Using a complicated assortment of dates and numbers, Camping sets out to show that his interpretation of "the infallible Word of God," uttered directly from God's mouth to scribes in the original languages of the Bible, gives proof that May 21, 2011, is the first Day of Judgment.

For most Christians any speculation about the end of time is a curiosity but no date is certain. If a Bible passage is referenced it is usually Acts 1:6-7. "Lord, is this the time when you will restore the kingdom to Israel?" Jesus replied, "It is not for you to know the times or periods that the

Father has set by his own authority." Passages from the 13th Chapter of Mark are also referenced regarding signs of the end of the age: "But about that day or hour no one knows, neither the angels in heaven, nor the Son, but only the Father." (vs. 32). If Jesus didn't offer or know a date, why should we designate one for him? Lifting apocalyptic passages out of context and applying them to another time and context only validates the futility of this kind of Biblical interpretation. If you start from the wrong premise you're likely to get the wrong answer.

Apocalyptic eschatology, dealing with "the end," unveils future events or the heavenly world. The context usually relates to events occurring at the time of their authorship. Chapters 7-12 in the Book of Daniel, although referring back to the Babylonian exile, relate to Antiochus Epiphanes of Syria and his persecution of the Jews which began in 168 B.C. The historical events surrounding "the little apocalypse" in the 13th chapter of the Gospel of Mark revolve around the destruction of the temple in Jerusalem in 70 A.D. The Revelation to John was probably written around the year 95 A.D. in the context of the persecutions of Christians under the Roman emperors Nero and Domitian. Using any of these sources to prove specific events in 2011 is to miss the point.

The end of time has been scheduled to occur many times. After the supposed day of Rapture has past, people go on about their business of daily living. In fact, that is the best way to live, to enjoy God's presence in the Now of our lives without becoming anxious about tomorrow. (Matt. 6:34)

An English Bishop while playing billiards was asked what he would do if he were told that he would die the next day. The Bishop relied, "I would finish this game of billiards which was begun to the honor and glory of God and will be finished to the honor and glory of God."

Perhaps that is good advice for us. Live each day to the honor and glory of God and let tomorrow take care of its own worries.

'Claim Your Joy'

With all the options we have to become depressed by alarming world events and personal challenges, it is good at the same time to look up and claim our joy. Our glasses can be half empty or half full. Our vision can look down or up. Our song can be in a minor or major key. We can stay with tears or smile with thankful hearts.

The Psalms express all of these emotions. Psalm 98 is one that expresses joy in the Lord.

"Shout with joy to the Lord, all you lands; lift up your voice, rejoice, and sing."

"Sing to the Lord with instruments – with harp, trumpets and the sound of the horn." "Let the sea make a noise, let the rivers clap their hands; and let the hills ring out with joy before the Lord." (Psalm 98:5-10)

The psalmist's hymn of praise is echoed in our own hymns. A text familiar to Episcopalians and members of the Church of England begins, "O praise ye the Lord." It is based on psalms 148 and 150. In the third stanza of this hymn praise is given to God with all things that give sound; "each jubilant chord re-echo around; loud organs, his glory forth tell in deep tone, and sweet harp, the story of what he hath done."

Contemporary worship continues the practices of our Hebrew ancestors, offering God praise and claiming our joy. While we worship in a variety of ways, both in music and silence, the sounding of instruments and the lifting of the voice in song are common practices in most traditions. God is praised in response to God's goodness and in thanksgiving for the wonders of creation. Even the rivers should clap their hands and the hills ring out with joy.

A few years ago my older son gave me an eight-day vacation with him in Hawaii. Hawaii was the only state in the union that I had not seen, so I looked forward to this new experience and the opportunity to share it with him.

Among the many wonders and beauty seen in Hawaii are the amazing contrasts that make up these islands. One morning I was enjoying sun and surf on the beaches of Mauna Kea, and that evening I was wrapped in a parka on top of Mauna Kea that reaches to a height of almost 14,000 (13,796) feet above sea level. It is the world's tallest sea mountain – 32,000 feet high from the ocean floor. From this spectacular height, where 14 international observatories scan the universe, we observed stars and galaxies billions of miles away. While looking I decided not to worry that the Milky Way and Andromeda galaxies are rushing toward each other for an eventual collision or merger since this won't happen for billions of years; and my sympathy for a ring nebula, a dying star, was relieved since its light will still be seen for many years to come.

These marvels brought the psalms to mind and I couldn't help but think of the splendors of God's creation that would inspire one to lift up voice and sing. The waves crashing on beaches were certainly clapping their hands and the hills were ringing out joy, cheering our hearts as we glimpsed the wonders of the universe. Sad to say, bad religion on occasion causes us to look through the wrong end of the telescope, thus limiting our perception of all that is and will be. We pick up the wrong end because we want finite answers to complex questions. But a more realistic view is to dare to glimpse the immensity of God's mysteries, to look up and out, or even to go the other direction into the mysteries of cells and genes and DNA that make us what we are. Such pursuits can be mind-boggling. It is the sort of thing that makes one want to "shout with joy to the Lord, to make music, to celebrate and give thanks."

Life will continue to be woven with woe and joy, but if we become discouraged, remember to pick up your small telescope and look through the small end to discover bigger dimensions of the wonders of God. Life is short, yet never too late to open our eyes to new wonders and to respond with shouts of joy. If singing and shouting aren't part of your nature, let your joy resonate in the quiet subtleties of your imagination. Let the deep peace of God's love warm your soul.

Humility

Jesus often turned things upside down. For example, in the parable of the Pharisee and the tax collector the "good guy" is the "bad guy" and the "bad guy" is the "good guy."

Jesus describes two men who went up to the temple to pray. The first one, a Pharisee, possessed all the usual qualities of righteousness. He said his prayers, fasted, and was not a "thief, rogue, or adulterer." When it came to the "Every Member Canvass," he tithed. The other fellow, a tax collector, had nothing to commend him. He failed where the Pharisee succeeded. But Jesus makes the tax collector the "good guy" and the righteous man the "bad guy." Why?

Jesus tells us that the issue is one of humility. The Pharisee did good works and had integrity, but he was locked into himself. He came before God to praise himself. His self-righteousness made him callous toward others; and like Little Jack Horner, he said, "What a good boy am I."

This scenario may be familiar to us. We are probably not guilty of parading our virtue. We exercise greater social refinement so as not to be open to ridicule. Nevertheless, we can maintain an internal arrogance that causes us to look at others with contempt.

Learning humility isn't easy. In the first place, we really are glad that we are not like some other people; and it's not a sin to give thanks for the gifts and talents God has given us. We are meant to be thankful; but a measure of our self-worth should not be based on the negative qualities of someone else.

False humility often gets in the way of true humility. Being self-effacing and subservient, as women and slaves were once expected to be, is a failure to respect the dignity of every person. That is not the kind of humility we should emulate.

It is also false humility to pretend that we don't have talents that we do have. There are singers, writers, and cooks who complain that they can't sing, write, or bake. Actually, this "I'm no good" approach is just an invitation to the beautiful music of contradiction from friends who say, "Oh, dear one, you have such a beautiful voice. Your articles are elucidative, and your English trifle is absolutely intoxicating."

This supposed humility is simply pride in disguise. As Sam Shoemaker, a famous preacher of the early 20th Century, said, "You can never have real humility while you are preoccupied with yourself; and an inferiority complex is the most self-centered state of mind in the world."

So what is real humility and how can we achieve it?

An approach to attaining humility is to evaluate our capabilities realistically remembering that all talents that we possess are gifts from God and are to be used for God's glory. "Real humility walks the fine line between self-criticism and self-acceptance." It has been said, "The soul that is truly humble takes its faults quietly and goes on afresh in confidence and hope." "You must not over-worry yourself about your advance in the Christian life either. It is simple – the love of God and love of people. That is perfection."

Humility in the biblical sense is a matter of one's relationship to God. "It is honest in self-evaluation. It is seeing ourselves as we really are – not as gods, but as human beings; not as super-heroes, but as sinners in need of the grace of God." This is what the tax collector realized and what the Pharisee failed to see.

Unfortunately, some of us learn humility only through humiliation. After being smug about our virtue we unexpectedly find ourselves saying, "mea culpa," my fault. It's not only politicians who are "found out." We all have a secret – and if that secret were known, we could be humiliated too. We can be thankful that most of the crimes of our hearts haven't been acted out; but we need to remember that we are capable of doing them.

It is not only in understanding our frailty that we maintain a semblance of humility; it is in a recognition that even our best efforts for good purposes may be used by God in ways that we may never imagine. When we give ourselves totally to God we may not achieve an anticipated goal but a greater work.

A great American 20th Century preacher once said that a good way to gain humility is not to seek it, but to cultivate a spirit of thankfulness – for happy events and even unhappy ones, seeking not for favoring circumstances, but for grace to meet all circumstances as God wants us to do it. When we do this, the more we are at leisure from ourselves, and therefore free to think about God and other people.

Patience

There are days when everything seems to go wrong. The car won't start, the checkbook won't balance, you've lost your cell phone and left it on vibrate so you can't call yourself to find out where it is. And then, when you return home after a busy day, you discover that your pedigree poodle hopped the fence to have a date with Heinz.

Daily problems are to be expected. When they occur our coping skills come into play. We may initially curb our frustrations with a moment of calm, or bunk the old adage, "Sit down and count to ten," as annoying advice. Some problems may even be life threatening, initiating a prayer to God for help.

James' advice to those suffering hardship is "to be patient until the coming of the Lord." (James 5:7-10) Maintaining allegiance to Jesus after his death was difficult for the disciples. Their expectation and hope was that the coming of the Lord to judge the earth would be soon. But as a seed takes time to produce fruit, they too had to endure suffering and maintain their faith in patience until fulfilled by the Lord himself. They were not to complain, nor judge one another, for the judge himself would come quickly.

Our approaches to problem solving may include this kind of patience without complaint or judgment. A tendency however, is to take charge of a difficult situation by ordering the lives of others as if they were our puppets. A preferable approach is to accept our problems as our own, perhaps even to welcome them as an opportunity for growth. When this approach is applied to our spiritual lives we discover that our Lord will indeed come to comfort us in our frustration, give us a deeper appreciation of God's love and mercy, and lead us forward to new possibilities.

James' advice to be patient is not a cure for the pain of problems, but it is an attitude that can shape the way we live and die – in the way we receive our Lord in life and death.

Many years ago I saw a television program about a young woman who became totally deaf. She needed ears to hear as someone blind needs eyes to see. For those contending with these problems trained dogs are often helpful.

Teresa, the deaf woman, chose a dog to be her ears. But instead of selecting a dog with superior hearing, she chose a dog that was deaf. The dog lived in her same silence. She taught the dog sign language so that it could respond, just as she had learned to communicate through signs. The dog learned to bark at special times just as she learned to continue her speech without hearing a word. By challenging her handicap with a positive attitude and by not succumbing to anger and frustration, she and her dog, with patience, learned to live positive lives and to be an inspiration to others. Instead of grumbling, making her life and that of those around her miserable, she transformed her handicap into a blessing of hope.

The negative counterpart of patience is grumbling; and when everything seems to go wrong, this may be our first reaction. Blame follows – some, perhaps, directed at God. We become intolerant of the imperfections of others. Grumbling becomes our recourse. If it persists, it can become a pattern of living – a habit most familiar. Should life improve, the next problem is quickly sought.

An inventor must envisage the finished product in order to choose materials and tools that will accomplish the task. And for Christians the finished product of what we shall become in Christ must always be in sight so that we don't lose track of our purpose for living and our destination. Being "patient for the coming of the Lord" may not involve his imminent second coming. It may simply mean that for the moment we are to be patient with the imperfections and frustrations of daily living so that we can find our real strength in Christ.

Beyond Words – The Holy Trinity

Trinity Sunday is the only Sunday in the Church Year dedicated to a doctrine rather than an event in Jesus' life. Knowing God in Trinity of Person, as Father, Son, and Holy Spirit, reiterates the faith of the Church declared by the Council of Nicaea in 325. This formula, from the twenty-eighth chapter of Matthew (vs.19-20), is the prescription used by Christians to initiate people into the Body of Christ and is the foundation for our creeds. God is understood to be one God in three persons.

While this doctrine is almost impossible to explain, it may be good that it is beyond our comprehension. God is beyond our comprehension, and descriptions of God always fall short. If they don't, we've described an idol, not God. God manages to be known by us but is not fully understood. We can proclaim that God is for us as a creating Father, was seen in Jesus, and that the Spirit of God is experienced in our lives. But that reality cannot be captured by words. We can just as easily refer to God as Creator, Redeemer, and Giver of Life. Those too are creedal words. To know God as a nurturing Mother is also valid. Julian of Norwich, the great English 14th century mystic, from her visions would express the nature of God not only as Father but as Mother. "As truly as God is our Father, so truly God is our Mother." Julian even spoke of "Jesus our true Mother in nature, from our first creation, and He is our true Mother in grace by His taking our created human nature." The Spirit too in Christian tradition is sometimes represented with feminine imagery.

This recognition that God is more than the words we use to describe God is a characteristic of Celtic spirituality. While boldly proclaiming God in Trinity of Persons, this God is enmeshed in the created order. God moves within creation. God is not a tree, but all living things express the wonder of the Creator. While a true image of God remains a mystery, we are nevertheless made in the image of that Mystery. The Divine Self is within all selves – within us, to be discovered and enjoyed.

We miss so much if we think of God only in religious language. God is meant to be experienced in every aspect of life, with or without a holy label. Beauty, for example is a gift from God and an expression of God's presence with us. We can see it, hear it, touch, smell, and taste it. As Philip Newell expresses it in a modern Celtic prayer:

"That in the elements of earth, sea and sky I may see your beauty; that in wild winds, birdsong and silence I may hear your beauty; that in the body of another and the interminglings of relationship I may touch your beauty; that in the moisture of the earth and its flowering and fruiting I may smell your beauty; these things I look for this day, O God, these things I look for." (*Sounds of the Eternal*)

The challenge for us is to look for God in all things. It is not enough to limit God to the confines of theological language. Unfortunately, trust in that discipline often leads to divisiveness. We tend to believe that our description of God is the only valid image, with the result that those who see God from a different perspective are designated heretics. We need to remember that the Divine Self lives even within those to whom we give bad names. God will not be corralled by doctrines, gender or racial imagery, ecclesiastical rules or rubrics. God is free to be known in all of life, to set us free from all that would bind us to destructive behavior and hopelessness. Traditionally we say that we have been set free from sin and death, discovered through the life, death, and resurrection of Jesus. And having received this grace through the Spirit, we then look into the sensitivities and wonders of God's presence "hidden deep in the palace of our souls" and in the gifts of creation.

To live in a relationship with the Holy Trinity is to enjoy the Creator in all the gifts of earth, especially in the love shared between persons. It is to discover our true selves as the Christ spirit becomes incarnate in our own lives. It is to be open to the mystical and ever moving winds of the Spirit that comfort, encourage, and challenge us to pursue a course that finds its fulfillment within the relationship of the Trinity.

In short, to live in relationship with the Trinity is to live within the reign of God's love. That love is not static but permeates all life, continually luring us to participate in the beauty of God. This is not primarily a matter of philosophical speculation. It is participation in divine action that is continually challenging and inspiring us so that we may move into intimacy with God.

One In Christ

In the Epistle to the Galatians we read that in Christ "there is no longer Jew or Greek, slave or free, male and female; for all are one in Christ Jesus." (Galatians 3:23-29)

This text is often quoted as witness to God's inclusive love for all people. The divisions of race, nationality, class, and gender that we use to separate ourselves from one another are not honored by God. As Christians we know too that we are united to one another in a special way by our baptisms. We are sisters and brothers in Christ. Jesus' stretched out arms upon the cross are a reminder that God's love extends to the entire creation.

While we may recognize this truth our trouble is putting it into practice. As we strive to treat one another as brothers and sisters in Christ we have to deal with our own fears and prejudices.

A look at history shows that Christians have endured many divisions. There was a time in first century Christianity when some thought that being a child of God was reserved for Jewish people. Later it was understood, especially with Paul's help, that the kingdom of God was open to Gentiles as well. While slavery existed, slaves were equally eligible for acceptance into the Body of Christ as were the free. Being male or female made no difference either. We recognize, however, that permission to perform certain functions within the church was not open to all. We still wrestle with that problem.

A look at history can be discouraging when one sees how Christians have fought against each other in religious wars, put one another to death because of differing beliefs, gone on crusades against people of other faiths, segregated believers because of race, etc. Even today some choose to determine who may or may not receive communion based on one's ethical and political agenda. I remember the days when divorced persons who remarried without the Church's permission felt alienated from receiving communion. I remember also as a child being told by an ethics professor that black people don't have souls in the same sense that white people have souls. We can give thanks that such a travesty is no longer taught.

The walls that we create to separate ourselves from one another are discouraging. And it is especially discouraging when we discover within ourselves prejudices we didn't know we had. Intellectually and theologically we may say that racial differences, for example, don't make any difference to God and shouldn't make a difference to us. But emotionally we may not be where our head is. I am grateful that in my own family we have a mixture of races and nationalities. Mayflower American, African American, Native American, Arab and English are all part of the mix. I even have dual citizenship. In this mixture I have discovered that it is much more difficult to exclude those who differ from one's self when they are a part of one's family. African Americans,

Native Americans, and Arabs are no longer "them." They, in fact, are me.

Edwin Markham in a poem has written:
They drew a circle that shut me out
Heretic, rebel, a thing to flout.
But love and I had the wit to win
We drew a circle that took them in.

Perhaps we need to learn how to draw big circles that encompass instead of circles and lines that separate. That is what Jesus taught. That is what Paul conveyed to Christians who were tempted to separate themselves from one another. That is what Love seeks to do for all of us – to help us see beauty in diversity, to bind up our brokenness, to draw us into community and make us one.

The Gift of Prayer

Prayer is often described simply as talking with God. One says words aloud or with quiet thoughts. The talking can be recitation of a formal prayer, such as The Lord's Prayer, or simple spontaneous thoughts expressed in thanksgiving, frustration, or as an appeal for help. Sometimes we may even think or say thoughts in anger, even at God. "Why didn't you keep my child from getting hurt on the ball field? Don't you see how this causes me pain?"

Prayer, of course, in order to be a conversation needs to allow time for listening – to hear what God might be saying. God needs a chance to answer your questions, to speak to your heart, and to surround you with grace. We often miss what God is saying to us because we don't quiet down enough to listen. This can be risky, however, because God might want to say something to us that we don't want to hear.

Ordinarily we think of prayer requiring words. Music and art can also express what we can't put into words. And fortunately, God understands our thoughts and emotions even when we are unable to express them in any form. God may even prefer for us to simply have the intention to be present for God without words, thoughts, or even emotions. Words may lock us into our thoughts and leave little room for God to speak to our hearts. Silence, after all, is God's first language.

Gandhi once said, "Prayer is not asking. It is a longing of the soul. It is daily admission of one's weakness. And so, it is better in prayer to have a heart without words than words without a heart."

God wants the deepest treasure of our lives – a loving heart filled with gratitude for the gift of life. And while our longing for God remains, especially in our weakness, God's longing for us is even dearer. Like a loving grandmother, God might wish to sit us on God's lap to fall asleep in a warm embrace.

Something More

Analysts continue to strive to understand why some people go to church and others don't. With declining membership in a number of mainline churches and significant growth in other religious bodies, analysts wonder what people want and what they don't want in their churches.

Some attribute the decline to those things that they are personally against. Others say not to worry about numbers if the Gospel is being preached and lived out in the life of a religious community. The growth of megachurches in recent years, which often concentrate on entertaining worship and programs ranging from Bible to bowling, might be considered the model for what every church should be doing. Yet others are saying that meeting the needs of a shopping mall society is not necessarily the way to build a community in Christ. Certainly, if we were to use Jesus' ministry as a model for success or failure, he was a failure during his life time. Most of his disciples abandoned him when the going got rough. But in the long run, billions have heard the message of God's love because of Jesus' witness.

Today, young people in particular refer to themselves as spiritual but not religious. They seem to identify with the spiritual aspects of their lives but don't have much interest in denominational orthodoxy. Coupled with this is a desire to feel good about one's self and to acknowledge a God who will improve one's lot in life. Some churches have shifted their focus to meet these needs.

Wherever you fit into this picture is not likely to have a big impact on your community; but in your own quiet way you may find quality of life as you live out your Christian vocation. Rather than assuming that God exists to make you happy, you can worship to acknowledge that God is worthy of praise. Many of us have met God's love in our lives and respond by giving thanks in worship, by following the pathway of love and service, and by seeking to live with God in the present moment. We recognize that self-indulgent enterprises will never satisfy. We do have needs, including forgiveness, healing, and new opportunities to lead positive lives. We proclaim the baptismal vows to "seek and serve Christ in all persons," "to strive for justice and peace among all people, and to respect the dignity of every human being." We do seek more than we have, especially a deeper relationship with God.

If we are looking for something more to fulfill our lives we may find it in the Biblical adage, "It is more blessed to give than to receive." (Acts 20:35) This wisdom should do more than make us feel guilty for being stingy. Giving and sharing is a truth worth pursuing in itself. Helping others puts us in relationship with those we serve. Love happens. God's nature is experienced in our lives.

Self-centered searches for happiness are bound to fail. If we are all get and no give, we become stagnant and no quality of life can live in us.

Francis of Assisi taught us much about the opportunity to be in relationship with God and others. As he prayed, "It is in giving that we receive." Forgiveness and pardon heal broken relationships. Compassion brings understanding and consolation. And his experience was one of joy, not sadness. He saw eternity in the present moment and led his life accordingly.

If you are looking for "something more" in your life, may you find joy in relationships through generous giving.

'It Ain't Necessarily So'

Since 1935 audiences have enjoyed George Gershwin's musical, Porgy and Bess. It has memorable songs including "Summertime" and "It Ain't Necessarily So."

"It Ain't Necessarily So" calls into question some Bible stories with the refrain, "It ain't necessarily so." Did David actually kill Goliath? Did Jonah make his home in the abdomen of a whale? Did Pharaoh's daughter find Moses in a stream? Did Methuselah live to be nine hundred and sixty-nine years old?

If one thinks of these Bible stories as historical events, "It ain't necessarily so" may be the correct response. There are many stories in the Bible that tell an important story that do not depend on the historicity of the characters and their actions. Just like good fiction, the circumstances of the story are usually not as important as the moral of the story, or its entertainment value, or its reflection on life experiences.

According to the story of Jonah, for example, Jonah was commanded by God to warn Nineveh in Assyria of its great evil and bring them to repentance. Jonah wanted to escape this responsibility, but after lamenting in the belly of the fish, he proceeded to do as God commanded and brought the Ninevites and their animals to total repentance.

One meaning of the story deals with Israel's mission, reluctantly embraced by Jonah, to preach God's divine mercy and the power of repentance. The story was interpreted allegorically by Jewish and Christian readers until more recent times when some wish to view even the stories in the Bible as literal truth.

One doesn't have to wonder if Jonah was swallowed by a big fish and then vomited alive onto dry land. That's not the point of the story. What is important is that God's mercy is universal, even if we are reluctant to proclaim it, and that each of us is called to turn around from the direction we may be going to find our true selves as we embrace God's love, mercy, and divine presence in life.

The Heretic and the Grand Inquisitor

Anthony de Mello tells the story of a prisoner confronting accusations against him before the Grand Inquisitor.

"Prisoner at the bar," said the Grand Inquisitor, "you are charged with encouraging people to break the laws, traditions, and customs of our holy religion. How do you plead?"

"Guilty, Your Honor."

"And with frequenting the company of heretics, prostitutes, public sinners, the extortionist tax-collectors, the colonial conquerors of our nation – in short, the excommunicated. How do you plead?"

"Guilty, Your Honor."

"Also with publicly criticizing and denouncing those who have been placed in authority within the Church of God. How do you plead?"

"Guilty, Your Honor."

"Finally, you are charged with revising, correcting, calling into question the sacred tenets of our faith. How do you plead?"

"Guilty, Your Honor."

"What is your name, prisoner?"

"Jesus Christ, Your Honor."

This story brings to mind the Inquisition of Medieval days when people were called before Church authorities to affirm their orthodoxy or to suffer severe penalties for heresy. The story is also a fine example of what happened to Jesus in his own day. Jesus was accused of violating Jewish law and tradition, of associating with drunkards, prostitutes, tax collectors, and public sinners, of criticizing religious leaders such as the scribes and Pharisees, even to calling them "whitewashed tombs." (Matt. 23:27) All of the accusations in the story are true to the Gospels.

Jesus was not always the nice guy. He was in fact a social revolutionary who taught how life should be lived if God were in charge. His prayer was that God's kingdom in heaven would be known and practiced in this life. His proclamation was both rejected and affirmed. He was brought to trial and suffered crucifixion. Yet, even today the good news of God's love for us, of our need to turn from destructive behavior to serve the good of others, is still proclaimed and affirmed.

Today the preacher, lay or ordained, can survive abuse in a safe environment. Yet, there are religious people dying for their faith in various parts of the world. The message is good but not always popular. Perhaps this is what Jesus meant when he said that one might need to pick up a cross in order to follow him. (Mark 8:34).

A Lease on Life

Years ago a friend of mine had a fender-bender. The accident was not his fault but he was left with the damage. I told him how sorry I was that this had happened to him. To my surprise, he said that the car was only a thing and that it and all the gifts of creation are only leased for awhile and then discarded or passed on to some else. Had he thought of his car as a possession the dent would have been an insult to his identity. But thinking of the car and all things as only leased helped him to be detached from possessions and to move on without regret.

We often think of happiness as the opportunity to accumulate many things and to claim them as "mine." This kind of individualism is popular these days. As is sometimes said, "The one with the most toys wins." But others have discovered that the best things in life need to be shared in order to be enjoyed – like love, peace, and the energy of life.

These qualities need to be given away to be received. The symbol of this generous spirit often includes the giving of things to others in need. What is "mine" is fine, but it might serve a better purpose to be given away. Why extend the lease beyond our need?

Questions some of us ask include: "Is my identity based on what I own? Is my self-esteem based on the adulation or envy of others? If I'm in a room by myself, is anyone there? When I die what will happen to those things I prepared for myself?"

Jesus had some thoughts on this subject. He said, "Take care! Be on your guard against all kinds of greed; for one's life does not consist in the abundance of possessions." (Luke 12:15)

It helps to live as my friend did – thinking of things not as personal possessions but as leased for a time to be shared with others. Even the "dents" in our lives can be diminished if we are detached from them as "mine."

God Looks Like You

What do you think God looks like? Some imagine that God is an old man with a long beard sitting on a throne ordering and judging the activities of the universe. He is usually thought to be benevolent, but must be obeyed if we hope to inherit eternal life in heaven.

Others think of God as if he were a policeman lurking to catch us in some offense. Guilty every day for our imperfections, we hide knowing ourselves to be bad.

Positive images include associations we have with names for God such as Love, Merciful One, Source of Life, Healer, Redeemer, Compassionate One, and the Tao (Way).

Paula D'Arcy, a spiritual writer, gives an intimate image of God. "God comes to you disguised as your life." Does that mean that God looks like me? Is God already inside of me participating in my life and I just can't see beneath the disguise? What about my neighbor?

31

Jesus taught that the kingdom of God is among us and within us. (Luke 17:21) St. Paul said that our bodies are temples of the Holy Spirit, a gift from God. (I Cor. 6:19) Even one of the stories of creation says that we were created in the image and likeness of God, male and female. (Genesis 1:27)

God has many images and at least one for each of us. While we may think of God being somewhere "out there," God's DNA is already planted within us. The challenge is to meet that presence.

If you want to know both God and yourself, unmask the Self that is sharing your life.

Living on Cruise Control

It has been said that 90 percent of people seem to live 90 percent of their lives on cruise control, which is to be unconscious. This can occur for people who follow their routines without reflecting on the meaning of their activities. The work they do defines who they are. Others cruise sticking to their values while refusing to undertake any new mental or spiritual challenges. Cruise control allows them to go forward without any turns or stops to deal with problems or to smell the flowers.

Perhaps the biggest problem living on cruise control is that it hinders our ability to discover who we really are. As Richard Rohr has written, "Life is a matter of becoming fully and consciously who we already are, but it is a self that we largely do not know." It is as if we had a giant case of amnesia that keeps us from discovering our true identity in God who dwells within us. "It is religion's job to teach us and guide us on this discovery of our True Self." The process is not a matter of earning merit badges to achieve an elitist status with God. God's love includes all of us. We are all children of God no matter what labels we attach to our beliefs and practices. God's True Self is present within us and can be awakened if we take time to turn, to stop, and to become conscious of the spiritual gene planted in us from birth.

Life is filled with many experiences, but sometimes we miss their deeper meaning. We look on the surface to see if they make us happy or sad. Like food, our bodies are satisfied or hungry. But the soul, the deeper essence of our identity, feeds on meaning to discover how it is connected to creation from its origins to the present moment. Being conscious of the Spirit praying in us is not likely to be discovered if we stay on cruise control. We have to take time to stop, to be silent, to listen, and to pray.

Maintaining a Friendship

Our relationship to God has been compared to a personal friendship. At first a new relationship may be experienced only as an acquaintance. Christmas cards might be sent each year to remember meeting one another. This friendship may develop, however, and the new friends begin to open their lives to each other and make a commitment to their relationship. This relationship may develop even more into intimacy and union with one another.

That is a model for our relationship with God. For some God is an acquaintance that is respected. Acknowledgement of the relationship may include grace before meals and prayers for one's family before bed. When the friendship develops the commitment may include regular worship and financial support to promote the mission of the faith. For others there is a longing to be united to God in perfect union. Intimacy with God is the desired commitment.

Wherever you may be in your relationship with God, maintaining the relationship requires acts of rededication. Love relationships don't stay loving or become intimate if the partners don't spend time together nurturing the relationship with renewed commitment.

For those of the Christian faith there are various prayers that can be said to recommit one's life to God on a daily basis. The one I use is by Ignatius Loyola (1491-1556). Perhaps you will find it helpful as you seek to nurture your relationship with God.

"Take, O Lord, and accept all my liberty; my memory, my understanding, and my will. Take me, and all that I have and am. You have given me all; behold, I restore all to You, to be disposed of according to your good pleasure. Give me only your grace and your love; this is sufficient for me; I will not ask anything else of You, but this."

E Pluribus Unum

The phrase, "e pluribus unum," has appeared on American coinage since the earliest days of our country. It was first used in 1795, appearing on the Half Eagle ($5.00 gold piece). The motto was suggested by the committee appointed on July 4, 1776, to design "a seal for the United States of America." From the Latin, the words are translated, "out of many, one." The motto alludes to the union between the 13 original States and the federal government as symbolized by the shield on the eagle's breast of the Great Seal. In 1956 the United States adopted as its official motto the phrase, "In God We Trust." This phrase has also appeared on U.S. coins since 1864 and on paper currency since 1957. The phrase comes from the Psalms. (Psalm 56:4)

"Out of many, one" also expresses the complexity of the people who make up this country. We come from many countries and cultures making this country our home. While we often honor the lands from which we came and the diversity of cultures, the aim is to share a common identity as one people under God.

For the most part we live up to this identity. But it hasn't been easy. African Americans, gays and lesbians, Native Americans, poor folks, recent immigrants, and others have suffered from prejudice and unequal justice over the years. Divisions within religious institutions have also been prevalent between Roman Catholics and Protestants, and more commonly today, between Christians and Muslims.

One would hope that if we cannot see God as the creator of all people who sees each of us as God's beloved child, that we could at least live up to mottos of our country that call us to be one people under God. We have a way to go to achieve "out of many, one," but with open minds and open hearts we may learn to see and accept one another as fellow citizens entitled to equal love and justice.

What Children Learn

Learning what life is about begins in early childhood. If you put your hand on a hot stove you're likely to get burned. If in a tender moment with an adult you are suddenly slapped, you know that love can't always be trusted. If in church you hear that you are going to hell if you don't come down front to get saved, you know that God is to be feared, not loved.

Dorothy Law Nolte writes that children learn what they live. "If children live with criticism, they learn to condemn. If children live with shame, they learn to feel guilty. If children live with approval, they learn to like themselves. If children live with kindness and consideration, they learn respect." She has nineteen of these "If children live" phrases that say so much about the way we should bring up our children.

Religion has the same responsibility to teach positive values. If the preacher is angry and mean spirited, we may think that God is mean too. If we hear only about sin, does that mean we are condemned, or is there any good news about forgiveness? If we hear that God is compassionate, aren't we likely to become compassionate ourselves? If we hear that God is the divine parent of all people, aren't we more likely to see one another as brothers and sisters? If love is our highest value, perhaps love is the energy we will most likely share.

Children and adults learn what they live. Pray that we may model good news to our children and to others.

Be Who You Are

Life is an adventure discovering who we are. Through interaction with others we seek a personal identity that can help us achieve a secure life with affection and esteem, and which gives us the opportunity to use our talents for the good of others and ourselves. Happiness is our goal.

In this search for identity, especially in community, we often accept the values given to us or that are imposed upon us. Happiness is sometimes achieved by not making waves. But an alternative is to leave home, so to speak, to find our identity apart from outside influences. Taking this action might seem rebellious, but each person must find his or her God given identity which is unique yet linked to everyone else.

Sometimes this search causes problems for those who have a predetermined idea of who we should be. A parent might wish that you become a lawyer or doctor, yet your enjoyment in life is in music and art. Do you vicariously live the parent's life instead of your own, or do you choose the path that meets your true interior self? Perhaps your struggle is not with other people's expectations of you, but with your own discernment of who you are. Perhaps the tension is coming to terms with your sexuality. A heterosexual orientation is not universal. For gay and lesbian persons acceptance of their sexuality can be stressful. Yet, in order to be honest to God one has to be honest to one's given self. We have to risk being the person God created.

A German mystic, Mechthild of Magdeburg (1208-1282), noted this clearly:

A fish cannot drown in water.

A bird does not fall in air.

Each creature God made

Must live in its own true nature.

God didn't make us all the same. We don't have to fit a single mold. If you feel like a fish, don't try to fly. If you feel like a bird, don't stay under water too long. God's spectrum of color for our lives is a full rainbow. Be your own color. Live your true nature. Be who you are.

It is in this honesty that the soul can encounter the divine, returning to God unashamedly the life the Creator gave.

That's Awesome!

If you have ever flown on a clear day or looked into the far distance from a high mountain, the sights you see may be truly awesome. When I fly to Alaska and see snow capped mountains, or view Denali in its grandeur, I understand what is meant by the phrase, "That's awesome." Younger people in particular use it frequently to express wonder or pleasure. And indeed, there are so many marvels in life that exclamatory phrases are appropriate to express the joy we experience in creation and the excitement of being alive.

Poets and composers have expressed their delight in word and song. The hymn, "For the beauty of the earth," is a combined art to give thanks to God for the earth and skies, for the love around us; for each hour of the day and night; for hill and vale, tree and flower, sun and moon, and stars of light. For the joy of ear and eye, for the heart and mind's delight, for the mystic harmony linking sense to sound and sight; for the joy of human love, brother, sister, parent, child; friends on earth, and friends above, for all gentle thoughts and mild. For all these things, to Christ our God we raise our hymn of grateful praise. (Text, F. S. Pierpoint)

Joy is the reward of time spent beholding the gifts of earth, sea and sky. To hear God's beauty "in wild winds, birdsong and silence... that in the moisture of the earth and its flowering and fruiting I may smell your beauty; that in the flowing waters of springs and streams I may taste your beauty. These things I look for this day, O God, these things I look for." (J. Philip Newell)

How Awesome!

Retelling the Stories

Children love to hear stories. Favorite stories are repeated over and over again. Sometimes the stories are told with embellishments adding anecdotes from family life.

Bible stories have been told the same way. Some people have assumed that the stories in the Bible were written down soon after the events they describe. But most of the Bible stories were carried down from generation to generation through an oral tradition. Some stories had their basis in historic events, and others were simply created to give meaning to human experience. The creation stories, for example, are not meant to be historical and scientific accounts of the method God used to create the universe. Rather, they tell the story that God is our creator and that we experience moral dilemmas of good and evil. Different cultures have their own stories that relate similar realities.

Many of the Hebrew Bible stories were not recorded until the time of the Babylonian captivity during the 6th century B.C.E. Even the New Testament books of the Bible were not written during Jesus' lifetime. St. Paul's letters are the earliest, probably written during the 50's. St. Paul didn't know Jesus personally, but experienced his voice and presence in a vision on the road to Damascus. Scholars don't believe that any of the authors of the Gospels knew Jesus personally since these writings date from the 70's to 100 C.E. Jesus died in the year 29. The average life expectancy was only 45 years.

While this recognition may be unsettling for some, the teachings and experience of Jesus' ministry were carried on by communities that gathered after Jesus' death. The stories continued to be told in the oral tradition incorporating interpretations of who the community believed Jesus to be and what his influence was on them. The stories, rather than intended to become rigid and set in stone, came to life again and again as the stories were told in the first century and have been retold for succeeding generations. Even today we don't tell the stories without giving them an interpretation. We adapt the stories to fit our present day experience so that the life of Jesus and other Biblical personalities can live again in our lives. In a sense there are no original stories, even if read from a common text. Each person who hears the story applies a personal interpretation. That is why Jesus so often taught telling parables.

Retelling the Bible stories is an ancient practice that can enrich our lives in the present day. Enjoy the good news you find.

Moratorium on Religion

A respected Christian educator and friend of mine once said that he would like to see a ten year moratorium on religion. The ministries of baptism and the burial of the dead should continue, but aggressive religious propaganda would cease. One could think theologically, but religious fanaticism would have a Teflon affect on gentle people. Political parties would not be pressured into adopting platforms that capture the narrow religious views of a militant few. Books and articles could still be written and read, just not banned or burned. Homegrown militia forces would not be fed by religious fear inciting them to prepare for their version of Armageddon, the last great battle of the forces of good against the government. Churches would no longer refuse to bury young people who die of AIDS. Silly modern versions of medieval hierarchical struggles over authority would cease. Progressive theologians would have permission to contemplate the mind of God and to relate their findings to their experience without fear of being condemned as heretics.

A review of western religious history tells a story of faith, but it is also a scandalous account of those, who in the name of God, have turned the Good News of Jesus into a shattering display of carnage. The tragic story begins with the killing of prophets and the crucifixion of Jesus. But the villains are not just those who stand outside the Judeo-Christian community. A look at medieval popes and their entourages is simple proof. Papal palaces, homes for the Vicars of Christ, became centers of intrigue. William Manchester writes, "The papal palace itself was often home to killers and their accomplices. Popes and cardinals hired assassins, sanctioned torture, and frequently enjoyed the sight of blood." (*A World Lit Only By Fire*, p. 37) Papal proclamations declared that the eating of meat on Fridays was a capital offense, that forgiveness for sins could be withheld unless expensive indulgences were purchased by the penitents. Bloody crusades and inquisitions turned baptismal waters red. Even 16th century reformers who protested against these errors of the Roman Catholic Church followed the decadent example of their former masters by seeking an "eye for an eye and a tooth for a tooth" in retribution. Such behavior, unfortunately, continues in religious wars to the present.

If this were the only true perspective of western religion, a ten-year moratorium would be too short. Call a permanent end to religion! Why join the hypocrites?

There is another perspective of Christian life through the ages, of course, that reveals divine light, not just the fires of witch hunts. That good story has been told over and over again by saints and heroes and simple folk like us. It is the story of Jesus' love and the freedom to live beyond the darkness of sin into resurrected life with God. It is the story of people who have turned their lives over to God and in the stewardship of their resources have brought good news to those in need. It is a story of feeding the hungry, healing the sick, and enlightening the ignorant. It is the story of people who have experienced a power greater than themselves, a Spirit that is both present and transcendent. It is the story of people who care about love, the conscience of the community, and who seek to be united with the Source of all being.

This tension of being faithful to God, of failing and striving to reform, is a persistent theme in the story we have inherited and to which we add the next chapter. Most of us won't call for a moratorium on religion, daring instead to profess a great Truth while making ourselves hypocrites.

The Ten Commandments

The story of the exodus under the leadership of Moses, and the giving of ethical and ritual laws to the people, is the basis of the covenant God made with the people of Israel. The Ten Commandments in particular have been an integral part of Jewish and Christian tradition and have even made their way into the public arena. Frequently we read about public debates to decide whether or not the Ten Commandments should be posted as art work in courthouses and schools, or in public spaces. Some think that having them displayed is pushing religion on people, who in this country are meant to enjoy separation of church and state. Others find the commandments to be neutral in character. They can be viewed simply as a code of ethics that is part of our culture and which may be observed or ignored.

For Christians the Ten Commandments are part of our Jewish heritage and continue to be moral guidelines for the living of our lives. In addition to the Ten Commandments, the laws given by God through Moses to Israel include six hundred thirteen laws that govern everything from upholding the Sabbath to celebrating Passover. "Many are highly specific rules, dealing with issues such as what foods may and may not be eaten, what the penalty is for cursing one's parents (death), what to do when an ox gores a person or another ox, what to do after an emission of semen, and so forth." (Marcus Borg, ref: Lev.19:18 (love neighbor), Exodus. 21:17 (death), Lev.11:1-47 (food), Exodus 21:28-36 (stoned), Lev.15:16-18 (discharge). These laws come from many different periods in Israel's history, having been accumulated over a period of centuries. The telling of the story in Exodus, Leviticus, and Deuteronomy is nevertheless associated with Moses at Sinai.

In the Ten Commandments, four tell us how to relate to God and six concern our relationship with others. God's covenant with Israel begins, "I am the Lord your God, who brought you out of the land of Egypt, out of the house of slavery. You shall have no other gods before me." As Marcus Borg points out, "The exodus story is not about social justice without God; equally, it is not about God without social justice." (*Reading the Bible Again for the First Time*, p. 105)

The exodus story of the delivery of Israel from slavery in Egypt, the giving of the law, and the forty years wandering in the wilderness before entering the promised land, combines historical memory with metaphorical narrative. There is no need to literalize the metaphorical narratives and try to figure out why God would send ten plagues on the Egyptians, how God parted the Red Sea for the people to cross on dry land, and then once they were safe on shore, drown the Egyptian soldiers pursuing them after Pharaoh changed his mind about letting the people go. To make Cecil B. DeMille's 1950's epic movie, "The Ten Commandments," a factual account of what happened thirteen centuries before Jesus is to miss the point. The story becomes incredible. If God acted that way then, why doesn't God do such things today in contemporary crises?

A preferable take on the story is to enjoy the story and realize that it is a story of liberation. We are meant to be free, and we are to be in a relationship of love with God and one another. The summary of the law says it so well: "You shall love the Lord your God with all your heart, and with all your soul, and with all your mind. This is the greatest and first commandment. And a second is like it: You shall love your neighbor as yourself. On these two commandments hang all the law and the prophets." (Matt.22:34-40)

The theme of promise and new life which is at the heart of Israel's story is our story too. Jesus' social ministry strove to lead us away from domineering empires that hold people in bondage, such as was experienced by first century Jews and Christians under Roman rule. Jesus' liberation teachings opposed economic exploitation by the wealthy, political oppression by the powerful few over the masses, and the attempts by religion to legitimize these abuses. The same issues that the people of Israel and Jesus dealt with in their day have not gone away. In this country the wealthy and mammoth corporations lobby against paying their fair share of taxes; money seems to buy elections so that the "chosen few" will have power to govern the poor and middle class; and God is used to validate the political agendas of religious extremists. These issues are current needing our assessment and action.

The work of social liberation and justice continues from Moses and Jesus to the present day. May our efforts to continue their ministries help to relieve oppression.

Pitiful, Just Pitiful

A friend of mine had a pet parrot. The parrot observed all her activities including her struggles dressing and undressing. On occasion when struggling with her socks, the pet would say, "Pitiful, just pitiful."

Indeed, some of her activities in old age were pitiful. But she enjoyed the humor her parrot gave to lighten the seriousness of her situation.

In our everyday lives we experience or meet others who live in truly pitiful situations. Some suffer severe illness and others disabilities. The word pitiful appropriately applies.

There are a variety of human conditions that seem pitiful but are not necessarily permanent, at least in an attitudinal sense. Many refuse to be overcome by their problems and choose to move forward with positive energy. Think of the blind who "see" with other senses and in their mind's eye. Think of paralytics who pursue college degrees and careers.

And think of those who have become accustomed to their pitiful lives and choose not to look out an open window to new possibilities. For some the "poor, pitiful, Pearl" syndrome is the means to receive sympathy and attention.

Why give up a good thing?

When Jesus healed a paralytic we don't know how much was physical disability and or perhaps psychosomatic. In any case, Jesus challenged the pitiful one to take a positive step. He said, "Take up your bed and walk." (Mark 2:1-12) The healing required not only Jesus' healing energy but a desire on the part of the paralytic to change. It required faith that a change was possible.

When we meet these challenges in our own lives, the specific desired change we pray for may not occur – the blind may not see or the paralytic walk – but the change occurs in one's response to their situation. They do not succumb to an identity of "pitiful," but develop skills and attitudes that benefit their lives and contribute to the welfare of others. Many assumed to be pitiful become fine teachers, musicians, scientists, parents, and lovers.

While none of us should thrust the responsibility for change solely on the pitiful to pick themselves up by their boot straps, our participation in their lives with love and care can sprout new growth bringing beauty to their lives and ours. God's healing presence is always available.

Light and Darkness

When I was a little boy and it came time for bed, my mother would read me a story, say prayers with me, and tuck me in; and then, turning off the light, she would close the door to my room. I felt loved. But I also remember that I was afraid of the dark. When I didn't think anyone was looking, I would sneak up to the door and open it, just a little, so that a tiny beam of light would come into the room. There was no real reason for me to feel insecure, but just having that little ray of light made me feel better.

Perhaps you or your children have had similar feelings. Seeing a light seems to say that everything is okay, even after we fall asleep. Light says that there is life. In the light our fears are relieved.

The anxieties and fears of childhood linger into our adult years. Even though we know that the sun doesn't cease to burn just because the sun sets, we nevertheless fear the powers of darkness. Light in both a literal and figurative sense has come to represent goodness and happiness. God is even seen as Light. But darkness, viewed as the empowerment of evil, threatens our walk. We feel insecure.

As symbols of our spiritual lives, light and darkness are equally powerful. We understand that God sent God's light into the world in the person of Jesus Christ. We celebrate that event at Christmas. John the Evangelist tells us that God is light and that in that light there is life. (John 1:1-14)

Even while knowing this there are times when the problems and disappointments of life are so severe that we fear there won't be a bright new day. These disappointments can weigh heavily on us, especially at holiday seasons when happiness is the expectation. But problems follow no convenient calendar. The seeming absence of God and the internal and external struggles and conflicts that we face can darken our outlook at any time.

Salvation from these problems is not just to lean and grow towards the light as plants do, but to learn to live in the darkness with confidence that the ultimate source of light, God, will not cease shining even when we cannot apprehend it. This was Jesus' experience at his darkest hours at Gethsemane and on the cross. Although he chose not to escape the grief and pain, he was able to conquer the darkness of death on a bright resurrection morning.

A friend who struggles with these issues wrote me a profound letter. He wrote of the powers of darkness but said that in his own life "ever so slowly, a blossom is budding in his consciousness; and like Samuel hearing a voice in the temple," he says, "Here am I, Lord." Because he had once seen the light he is able to live in the darkness. To do this requires faith and trust. But it is faith and trust in the Source of light that can bring us into a closer relationship with God. My friend writes, "And maybe soon I'll be blessed with the strength to let go and sail with joy into the darkness, knowing that trust and faith are the servant's tools."

Imagine sailing into the darkness with joy. That, in fact, is the experience of some of the greatest lovers of God. While God is not darkness and emptiness and nothingness, the experience of God is often found in darkness and emptiness and nothingness. One enters into the void, into a cloud of unknowing which seems like nothingness. One might even feel abandoned by God, left high and dry with God absent. But in the emptiness the void may be where God is. One discovers that the God who seemed absent was present all the time. The darkness turns to light. As light blinds the bat or as excessive light of the sun blinds the human eye, so the excessive light of God plunges us into thick darkness.

Indeed, this is a lesson the child of Bethlehem came to teach us. As he lived in the light of his heavenly Father, so was he able to be secure in the darkness. That hope is ours also.

The Holy Family

Christmas is a time for stories. Beloved tales of the season are told over and over again. Children and adults alike have their favorite stories and enjoy hearing the mystery and magic of Christmas retold.

The most famous Christmas story, of course, is that of the birth of Jesus. Accounts of his birth are told in the first two chapters of the gospels of Matthew and Luke. Matthew's narrative tells of Joseph's obedience to the message of the angel that he should take Mary as his wife and name the child conceived in her womb, Jesus. It is a story that touches our hearts as we remember that it is God's pleasure to be with us. The compilers of the birth narratives not only told this good news but found it important that any accusations against Jesus, that he might be illegitimate, be covered by the explanation that his conception was by the Holy Spirit. They also needed to express their faith that Jesus was more than just a man. With God as his father and Mary his mother, divinity and humanity were united in one person.

Although there are many similarities in the Matthew and Luke accounts, Luke has Mary responding to the message of the angel instead of Joseph. Mary is told that she is not to be afraid, for she had found favor with God, and the child conceived in her womb would be the Son of God.

These stories, which are primarily non-historical dramatizations of the birth of Jesus, are faith statements designed to make Jesus' origins intelligible against the background of the fulfillment of Old Testament expectations. They are stories to tell us that those who experienced the Christ believed that Jesus was the long awaited Messiah, the one sent from God to save us from sin and to give us new life and hope. They are stories to tell us that God came to us in a simple fashion to incorporate even the least of us into God's life and to give us a vision of God's kingdom that will lead us from this life to the next.

One of the aspects of the birth narratives that I enjoy most is the way they give us an idea of what our relationship to God is meant to be. I am moved by the obedience of both Mary and Joseph to follow the message of the angel even when it involved risk. For both Mary and Joseph there was the scandal of Mary being pregnant before they were married, and that the child was not Joseph's. While the purpose of this aspect of the story is to show the unity of the divine and human natures of Jesus, it can also mean for us that there are times when following the demands of God's love puts us at risk. Debates regarding social and human justice issues often challenge our morality when it comes to respecting the dignity of every person. Obedience to God can also mean that there may be times in our lives when we like Mary and Joseph will find no "room in the inn" to birth the God in us. That was Jesus' experience from his birth in Bethlehem to his death on Calvary. The love of God incarnate in his life found little room in most people's hearts. That is also the risk we take if we choose to be Jesus' disciples. Submitting ourselves to Divine Love as Jesus did may not find for us a worldly kingdom.

It is, however, in offering ourselves completely to this Divine Life that our souls can find their greatest fulfillment. Joseph said "yes" to the Spirit, and although we know little about his life, we understand that he forfeited his more cautious self in order to be an instrument of God's good pleasure. Mary also said "yes" to God, and although initially fearful, she made the purest and simplest commitment to the will of God, which literally took over her whole being. Her surrender to God meant that humanity and divinity would be incarnate not only in her child but in her as well.

Mary's example can be the model or prototype of what is meant to happen spiritually in each of us. Whether female or male we all are meant to become pregnant virgins, so to speak, to welcome into our humanity the Spirit of God. It is the process of discovering within our own humanity the union of soul and body with God. Like a physical pregnancy there is wonder regarding the nature of the child to be born.

We wonder what it is that God will choose to birth in us. There is usually risk and pain in these pregnancies. Even the water and blood can become for us the symbols of our life in Christ, the waters of baptism that give us birth into a new relationship with God as God's children, and the blood of sacrifice that can be the cost of following the demands of love. Yet, by allowing the seed of God's love to be conceived in us, we can discover an incarnation of the Spirit that will shape us into the image of God and produce fruits of goodness and love. It is a surrender of our hearts to God that arouses our spirits, and while unpredictable and mysterious, produces joy. The relationship carries us through our doubts and perplexities because our ultimate trust is not placed in our own resources but in the power of God to take our frail natures and create new life within us. We become wedded to the Spirit, relinquishing our own private desires so that we may submit ourselves to the divine action of God. Love lures us to commit our whole being to God so that we may become temples of the Holy Spirit. By surrendering our lives to God the kingdom we seek becomes the treasure we bear in our bodies.

The Blessed Virgin Mary

Much of the action of God in Christ that we celebrate at the Advent/Christmas seasons can be seen through the life of the Blessed Virgin Mary. By her willingness to be the mother of Jesus we are able to see the unity of the divine in humanity. Divine love is born through a human mother. The God of creation enters into our humanity in a unique way through the life, death, and resurrection of Jesus.

According to the birth narratives, Mary accepted the power of God in her life which symbolizes for us the cooperation needed to participate in a loving relationship with God. Mary conceived Jesus not only in her womb but in her heart. And whereas Jesus is not conceived physically in our lives, we are offered the gift of grace to receive Christ into our hearts. As Mary said in response to the angel Gabriel, "Here am I, the servant of the Lord; let it be with me according to your word," (Luke 1:38) so is her acceptance meant to be our response as we live into a relationship with God.

Some see Mary's acceptance of her role as a passive relationship to God rather than taking an active role of cooperating with God in the work of salvation. Our tendency to see Mary in a passive role is a reflection of the Judaeo-Christian tradition of expecting passivity on the part of women in a masculine dominated society. It is the expectation that women are to take the inferior role often portrayed in the Hebrew Bible and characteristic of first century Judaic culture. This unfavorable expectation is reversed in the New Testament where a woman is honored above all others for her role in God's plan of wooing our love. The oppression that women have received, as if they had not been created in the full image and likeness of God, is redeemed. The cooperation of Mary to birth Jesus is an active willingness to participate in the purposes of God.

This cooperation required humility not passivity. It required the emptying of commitments and hurtful things that might hinder her relationship with God. It required patience and meekness. Later St. Paul would describe what cooperation with Love entails. He wrote, "Love is patient; love is kind; love is not envious or boastful or arrogant or rude. It does not insist on its own way; it is not irritable or resentful; it does not rejoice in wrong doing, but rejoices in the truth." (I Cor. 13:4-6)

The truth that we have come to understand regarding the unity of humanity with divinity is seen in the birth of Love at Christmas. God became empty and humble to bring humanity into a closer relationship with the Godhead. God's action did not force Mary's acceptance of her role in this plan nor is acceptance of our relationship with God demanded. We can accept Love or let it go; yet, God's love for us remains true in either case.

Mary was able to magnify the presence of God in her life. She expressed this in the worship of her song: "My soul doth magnify the Lord, and my spirit hath rejoiced in God my Savior. For he hath regarded the lowliness of his handmaiden. For behold from henceforth all generations shall call me blessed." (Luke 1: 46-55) She experienced the wonder of her role in the birth of Jesus and in her continuing vocation to be faithful to her son from his birth to his resurrection.

In a sense we all have Mary's vocation. We are meant to bear Christ in our bodies and to bring to birth an outward expression of that presence that magnifies God to others. When this happens, the incarnation is not limited to a moment in time or to one God-man. Instead, God in Christ becomes the prototype of all that is meant to be awakened and lived within each one of us.

A Fork in the Road

At the beginning of a new year many make resolutions to improve the quality of their lives. After an abundance of holiday food and good cheer some will undertake exercise programs and a diet. These good intentions may include becoming a better parent or spouse, giving more to charity, or taking a journey down a new path of life.

Sometimes the ensuing journey meets a fork in the road. Should I turn left or right? Where will each lead?

Yogi Berra, the baseball legend, had a simple solution. "If you come to a fork in the road, take it." Whether or not his wit is nonsense or wisdom, when we meet a crossroad in life it is important to take it. Mark Nepo has written that when we meet a fork we shouldn't stall too long and "hesitate our way out of living. We can't experience everything, and taking one road will always preclude another, but agonizing over which to take can eventually prevent us from knowing any road."

Some people fear making a mistake. Instead of looking at life as an adventure to discover God's hand in all of creation, they think of life as a matter of do's and don'ts as if God had a long list of requirements for us to satisfy with A+ achievement. Such a view of life makes a fork in the road a scary proposition. If I take the wrong turn I'm guilty and God will be mad at me. Perhaps on moral issues when we willfully choose to do what is contrary to love, this probably applies. But often the circumstances of life are left to our free choice. Be who you are. If you discover that the turn you took leads in a direction you don't want to go, turn around or use your spiritual GPS (God Prayer Service) to recalculate your direction so that you can find the peace and fulfillment you desire. There is no need for guilt. Jesus' message was to free us from guilt – you are forgiven, move on. If your first choice doesn't work, take the alternative. Taking ourselves too seriously leads to spiritual pride. Have the humility to accept your humanity and to be generous to others without judgment when they take a turn that needs re-routing.

God is with us all the time. God has searched us out and knows us. God follows our paths and is acquainted with all our ways. At the fork of any road, God is with us whichever way we turn. (See Psalm 139)

Love Poems from God

Saints and poets have written poems as if sent from God. I have several collections and find them inspirational, drawing me closer to a love relationship with God. Characteristic of these poems is that they have little to do with heaven or hell, a favorite topic for the public in 2011. Rather, they adore God for God's sake. One doesn't love God in order to be saved. Whatever the afterlife may be, God is worthy of praise now as we offer our minds to know God, our hearts to love God, and our bodies to glorify God.

I especially enjoy the love poems of St. John of the Cross (1542-1591). He is recognized as one of the world's great mystical poets. Here is a short poem entitled, "I Am What is Loved."

I said to God, "What are you?"

And He replied, "I am what is loved. I am not what should be loved for how cruel that would then be for my bride."

We are the beloved of God, the bride, seeking to consummate our love in union with the source of all love. God doesn't demand our love, for that would be cruel. Love must come from free choice. This Lover sees more good in us than we can see in ourselves or others, for the Beloved only "sees Himself" in us. If we get carried away seeing only what is wrong with ourselves, others, and the world, pray to see with God's eyes who sees light flickering within us even in our darkness.

Love poems can even be humorous. St. Teresa of Avila (1515-1582), a great contributor to spiritual literature and poetry, wrote that some of us may not have been tickled by God. Here is her poem, "Not Yet Tickled."

"How did those priests ever get so serious and preach all that gloom? I don't think God tickled them yet. Beloved hurry."

Too much gloom and doom from the preacher may say more about the anger in the preacher than the joy found in God's love. As Thomas Merton has written, it sometimes happens that people "who preach most vehemently about evil and the punishment of evil, so that they seem to have practically nothing else on their minds except sin, are really unconscious haters of other people. They think the world does not appreciate them, and this is their way of getting even." Perhaps such folk need to be tickled by God.

The message of the Beloved to us is, "Enjoy Me."

Agreeing with Atheists

On occasion you may meet someone who says, "I don't believe in God." If you are a religious person, you might at first be taken aback. You might think to yourself, "Poor soul. It's a shame that such a lovely person will spend eternity in hell." If you are of an evangelical bent, you may attempt to "rescue the perishing" even in an aggressive fashion. Centuries ago missionaries in Latin America would baptize babies and then smash their heads in so they would go to heaven immediately. A friend of mine calls this sort of evangelism, "getting scalps for Jesus."

My response to people who say they don't believe in God is to ask them to tell me about the God they don't believe in. Often they have learned a distorted image of God that has driven them away from Christianity. They may have been told that God is a man with a long white beard sitting on a throne in heaven judging every move we humans make. This God, usually called Father (feminine characteristics are usually suppressed), loves us only if we obey him according to the Bible, as if the Bible miraculously dropped out of heaven in the King James Version. They think believers claim to have everything figured out, including scientific proof from the Bible that the universe was created in six literal days just as the Bible says. It is a curiosity for them that God would make light before creating the sun, moon, and stars. (Genesis, Chapter 1)

As the conversation continues I find that I don't believe in the God they don't believe in either. Turning myth into history and science can turn off any educated person. Yet, this misunderstood image of God is often the belief of many dedicated Christians who turn off their minds thinking that taking these things on "faith" is a sign of faithfulness to God. Meanwhile, such believers usually have an internal sense of the presence of God in their lives while holding biblical misinformation. For the atheist the opposite is true. The atheist may have valid skepticism of believers' claims, but lacks that inner sense of the presence of God. Such a person often looks for a God "out there" and can't find one worthy of worship. All along the God of the universe is to be found within one's own life. The trick is to let go of the false self we have nurtured to achieve security, affection, power and control, to discover the true self within that is a reflection of the great Mystery to which some of us subscribe.

When you find yourself agreeing with atheists, don't scold yourself. Listen to what they have to say. Help them process their thoughts without judgment. Look for the buried Christ within them awaiting resurrection.

Is God Like a Cow?

I had an awakening by friends who told me how important a cow can be. They told me about a cow that sold for $53,000. The importance of this cow is linked to the eventual genetic make-up of a herd. I knew that cows were valuable for milk and meat but didn't realize their value for financial advantage.

This education reminded me of something Meister Eckhart (1269-1329) wrote. He was a priest and spiritual genius of his time. He said, "Some people, I swear, want to love God in the same way as they love a cow. They love it for its milk and cheese and the profit they will derive from it." He went on to say, "Those who love God for the sake of outward riches or for the sake of inward consolation operate on the same principle. They are not loving God correctly; they are merely loving their own advantage."

I imagine we have all fallen into that trap. We go shopping for God to gain some personal advantage as if we were looking for a bargain on Black Friday. We may seek a relationship with God considering first what we can get out of the relationship rather than what we can put into it. In some circles the reason for loving God is to avoid the fear of hell. Loving God is no more than fire insurance.

Looking for personal gain in a relationship with God was not Jesus' message. He said that loving God and our neighbor could be costly. For him it led to a cross. He lived in his life and death a commitment that love is our highest value, demonstrated through forgiveness, and that love is the nature of God who is the source of all life.

Certainly for Jesus a cow is important, but not as a model of what God can do for us as if we owned a $53,000 cow. We love God because God first loved us (I John 4:19). We give thanks to God for the gift of life, for the miracle of creation, and for the joy of relationships lived with love. But we do this because God is worthy of praise. Love for God is more than "loving our own advantage."

Spiritual Imperialism

Mohandas K. Gandhi (1869-1948), the hero of the Indian independence movement, was a deeply religious person. While maintaining his participation in the Hindu faith he was greatly influenced by the teachings of Jesus. The Sermon on the Mount and Jesus' nonviolent approach to dealing with conflicts was of particular importance. "Love your enemies and pray for those who persecute you." (Matthew 5:44) It was this nonviolent approach that he applied to political struggles that won independence for India from Britain.

Gandhi was not enamored, however, by those who claimed that to appreciate Christianity one had to take on the customs of Western civilization and Christian dogma. An aggressive attempt to make everyone conform to a narrow spiritual expression, at the expense of other traditions, was for Gandhi a form of spiritual imperialism. It marred his appreciation of the "beauties of Christianity."

Some who express enthusiasm for their particular faith and practice often forget that everyone comes from the Source of all being. God is not just the God of Gentile Christians. In fact, Jesus did not intend to found a new religion. He was a Jew, his disciples were Jews, and he died a Jew. It wasn't until years after his death that his followers became a Jewish sect finding their spiritual strength in the teachings of Jesus rather than in the leadership of the Pharisees and Sadducees.

Attempts to funnel the Mystery of God into one uniform set of beliefs (dogma), a book (Bible), or in a sacrament (Communion) produce idols that can't be fully trusted. The spiritual journey requires humility, a willingness to listen and to appreciate the experience of others. Spiritual imperialism is not a valid mission strategy. It only separates people into unhealthy divisions. We are all children of God regardless of label.

Don't Let the Past Steal the Present

During the second half of life one tends to reflect on times past. Nostalgic memories are retrieved and remorse is felt from echoes of failed relationships and unaccomplished hopes. One may be grateful for a good life or mired in disappointments. With each new day comes a chance for learning and delights or a struggle to postpone the placement of life's last piece of the puzzle – death. At age twenty-five there seem to be fifty more years to create a rich legacy. At seventy-five the accolades are just a memory. "What might have been and what has been point to one end, which is always present." (T.S. Eliot) The future is suddenly now.

Those who linger in memories and remorse tend to let the past steal the present moment. Energy to recover or change the past blurs the miracle of a new day. One might ask, "Am I already dead in spirit or does a mini-adventure await me to bring a thankful heart?"

St. Paul wrote that we should "Rejoice in the Lord always." (Philippians 4:4) He certainly had innumerable hardships to regret, but he moved forward rejoicing in God's presence in his life. He didn't let the past steal the present moment.

Everything that has been points to the present moment. It can be treated as a dead end or an unfolding of new patterns for rejoicing.

Walk the Talk

The slogan "Walk the talk" reminds us to practice what we preach. Whether a preacher or not, the example of our lives is usually worth more than many pious words. Good words not practiced align us in the company of hypocrites, a fall we hope to avoid.

Recently a friend and I had dinner at a Japanese restaurant. The young waiter was from Tibet. Tinly had a gentle and courteous manner, and even bowed slightly to us when we said thank you. Coming from Tibet we asked if he is a Buddhist. He replied that he is. We asked him a few questions about that way of life. He told us about his prayer at home which supported his desire for peace and the release of anger. Compassion was at the heart of his practice.

I was impressed that this young man revealed such a beautiful message through his person as a waiter. He walked the talk with only a few accompanying words to respond to our inquiry. Being a recipient of this goodness was a blessing and a welcome relief from the hostile political bashing swelling the media. I was reminded that mean-spirited harangues even from preachers do not witness to the fruits of the spirit St. Paul encouraged us to seek: Love, Joy, Peace, Patience, Kindness, Generosity, Faithfulness, Gentleness, and Self-Control. (Galatians 5:22-23) Walking the talk says more than ten thousand words.

Who Cares?

In a Faith and Values article in The Tennessean, religion columnist, Ray Waddle, noted that a LifeWay Research study found that 46 percent responding to the survey said they never wonder whether they will go to heaven. Asked about the question, "How can I find more meaning and purpose in my life?" 28 percent said they never think about it.

In the post Christian era in which we live, questions of meaning and purpose relating to religion are dwindling. Attendance at traditional denominational churches is decreasing. The ethos of emotional and spiritual support found in many congregations is often limited to older members; and the imperative to evangelize the "good news" is losing its power. People who have little concern with philosophical or religious involvement tend to be courteous to those who have these concerns, but their personal response to such speculation would probably be, "Who cares?"

Spiritual indifference has given way to athletic and other entertainments, technological toys, consumer consumption, and a "me first" approach to life. While some young people still ask the age-old questions of purpose and meaning, it is usually those in the second half of life who become more concerned about spiritual values. As one approaches death, speculation about an afterlife comes to mind. "Has my life thus far made a difference to anyone? Who thought up the miracle of life in the first place? Is there more to come? Do answers to these questions make any difference or are they just curiosities to ponder in idle moments?"

There may be comfort for those who still ask these questions to know that spiritual concerns ebb and flow in each generation. In fact, seasonal cycles are not only a part of creation but are cycles in our thinking giving opportunities for values to be reviewed and renewed. What is slipping now may need to be released so that vibrancy can return to life again. A lobster, for example, has to lose its hard, crusty shell, and become vulnerable to the elements in order to grow a new and stronger body. Perhaps that is the positive side of what is currently going on in our society. Opportunities for renewal are plentiful. Meanwhile, ultimate questions are still appropriate to ask even if answers leave us with a deeper sense of humility.

Abraham

The three great monotheistic religions, Judaism, Christianity, and Islam, claim a common father – Abraham.

Abraham was the first person in recorded history to understand that there is only one God. We read about him in the Book of Genesis. God says, "I will make you exceedingly fruitful; and I will make nations of you, and kings shall come from you. I will establish my covenant between me and you, and your offspring after you throughout their generations, for an everlasting covenant, to be God to you and to your offspring after you." (Genesis 17:1-7, 15-16)

This came somewhat as a surprise to Abraham since he had no children by his wife Sarah. Yet, we hear that God would provide a son for them even in their old age. That son was Isaac. And from Isaac came Jacob; and from Jacob the twelve tribes of Israel. This is the Biblical heritage for Jews and Christians.

Islam also has a claim to Abraham, but rather than tracing their heritage through Isaac, their relationship to Abraham comes through Ishmael, Abraham's first son. Ishmael was the son of Sarah's maid, Hagar. Tradition says that Abraham took Ishmael to Mecca where Ishmael married an Egyptian woman and became the father of twelve tribes himself. These tribes are associated with Bedouin tribes around the Middle East from the late first millennium B.C.E. Ishmael is identified as the progenitor of the Arabs.

While the tradition and folklore of Abraham and the patriarchs of Israel date back to 1996-1690 B.C.E., Abraham was a product not of the time that the story took place but of the time the Old Testament scriptures were written down in the 6th century B.C.E. when the Neo-Babylonian Empire ruled the world. Prior to that, the stories were carried on from generation to generation through oral tradition.

When we translate this common heritage into modern times we see how difficult it has become for descendants of Abraham to reach common ground regarding the Holy Land. Each one claims that the area encompassing Israel and Palestine is their inheritance from their father Abraham. Jerusalem, in fact, is a center for all three religions. What is known as the Rock is said to have been the place where Adam was buried. Solomon built the Temple there. Jesus prayed there and it was from the Rock that Muhammad ascended.

Jerusalem has been called the Navel of the world. The remains of the Temple, which was destroyed in 70 C.E., is known now as the Western Wall where devout Jews and other religious people often pray. Jesus was crucified in Jerusalem. And the Dome of the Rock is the third holiest mosque in Islam.

For many centuries adherents of each religion have fought over the land. The legacy is one of blood: Muslim/Jewish warfare; Christian/Muslim warfare. The animosity between Arabs and Jews continues to this day. And since as Christians we have a Jewish heritage, we are likely to be on the side of Jews and opposed to Muslims. We see anti-Muslim attitudes even in this country with Muslims labeled as terrorists and protests surrounding the building of mosques.

Perhaps in a small way we could pray and promote an attitude of compassion for one another rather than succumbing to attitudes of divisiveness.

Christian compassion means "to suffer" with someone. It bids us to go where people hurt and to enter into their pain – to be present for them, and when possible, to help. Judaism bids us to repair a broken world by performing acts of mercy and kindness. Islam reminds us that what God has to say to us is informed by both mercy and compassion, and thus it becomes our responsibility to speak and act in the name of God the Merciful, the Compassionate One.

It isn't in our power to repair the whole world, but in small ways we may be able to promote the goodness each religion has to offer, and learn to honor those of other faiths as we claim with them Abraham as our father.

A Dark Day

During the Lenten season many Christians walk the Way of the Cross. They reread the passion stories and reflected on Jesus' life and death in their thoughts and prayers. And then they commemorate Jesus' death on that first Good Friday with petitions that set his passion, cross, and death between God's judgment and our souls.

On Good Friday we find ourselves in the company of transgressors, of those who condemned Jesus, who ordered the crucifixion, and who died on either side of him. The evil of this world and its cost seem very close. And we find ourselves not just as bystanders who look in on these events, but as those who have also failed or lost our way. While we weren't at the cross to hammer nails or thrust a spear, we know that our own sins need the healing of outstretched arms to embrace us with forgiveness.

Edwin McNeill Poteat in a poem reminds us that the passion of Jesus is not to be forgotten when the hosannas of Palm Sunday are over. It is entitled, "Palm Sunday and Monday."

They pluck their palm branches and hail him as King,
Early on Sunday;
They spread their garments; hosannas they sing,
Early on Sunday.
But where is the noise of their hurrying feet,
The crown they would offer, the scepter, the seat?
Their King wanders hungry, forgot in the street,
Early on Monday.

That early on Monday is now the following Friday. The palms have turned into whips. The hosannas are cries to crucify. We enter the devastating and glorious absurdity of the sinless one identifying with us in our faults – who honors our hosannas, and who lifts us up even when we forget. If we do remember, we take to heart Jesus' call to us to take up our crosses too – to be the help and hope for others who forget early on a Monday.

Jesus, the Civil War, and the Titanic

Daniel Mendelsohn in a New Yorker article quoted a historian who said, "the three most written-about subjects of all time are Jesus, the Civil War, and the Titanic." The statement may not be true but isn't much of an exaggeration. All three have inspired hundreds or more books, articles, novels, and dramatizations, and they continue to fascinate the public. Questions regarding all three continue to be asked. Those in search of the historical Jesus might ask, "Will the authentic Jesus please stand up?" Is the historical Jesus the important search or is the Christ of faith what we really want to understand and experience? Civil War buffs still research the causes of the war. Numerous theories abound and tend to reflect a regional perspective. And now with the 100th anniversary of the sinking of the "unsinkable ship," more is being written about the Titanic, and a 3D version of the 1997 blockbuster film has been released. Questions considered include wondering why the reporting of the iceberg was so late, leaving only a minute to spare before the collision?

Many comparisons can be made of these three disparate historic events, but it may be the similarities that have created such widespread interest. Apart from their appeal to adventure, each deals with life and death. Who will be saved? Who goes to heaven and who doesn't? In war, whose God is on the winning side? In a disaster, who will be rescued and who will drown?

All three deal with class and race. Using the class strata on board the Titanic, who was permitted to get into the life boats first – the upper-crust privileged in first class, or poor Irish emigrants in steerage? In the War did the South have the moral right to protect their property – slaves; or as a nation do "we hold these truths to be self-evident, that all men are created equal, that they are endowed by their Creator with certain unalienable Rights, that among these are Life, Liberty and the pursuit of Happiness?" With Jesus do the poor deserve the same dignity and benefits of the rich? Was not his mission "to preach good news to the poor – to proclaim freedom for the prisoners and recovery of sight for the blind, to release the oppressed, to proclaim the year of the Lord's favor?" (Luke 4:18-19)

The kinds of questions arising from these three themes continue to be asked on a variety of levels. They are issues deserving reflection in our attempts to make sense out of life. They conjure up human and moral dilemmas we face in our own day, and bring us face to face with tragedy. Jesus was crucified. At least 618,000 Americans died from the Civil War. More than fifteen hundred passengers and crew sank with the Titanic.

Jesus, the Civil War, and the Titanic remind us to live our lives fully while being sensible of the shortness and uncertainty of life. They also remind us to live each day as if our last, and not to miss the beauty, awe, and wonder of being alive.

Science vs. Religion

Some people pit science and religion against each other as if they were incompatible. For example, the first story of creation in the Bible says that God created the universe in six days and rested on the seventh. The prevailing scientific explanation of what happened at the beginning of our universe, however, is the Big Bang Theory. This theory does not mean that there was a big explosion, but our universe came into existence as a "singularity" 12 to 15 billion years ago and continues to expand. Another example is that prior to the 16th century most people thought the earth was flat and that the sun orbited the earth, until Galileo demonstrated that the earth is not the center of the cosmos. Meanwhile, the Roman Catholic Church regarded the explanations by Copernicus and Galileo as heretical, contradicting the doctrines of Holy Scripture. It took 300 hundred years before the Church changed its mind.

Religion is not the only discipline with blinders. There are those who disregard religion altogether believing that everything that is must be verified by the empirical method which requires experimentation and observable proof. The scientific method, however, is too limited in its scope to grasp matters of the Spirit. In fact, the things that make life worth living, such as experiences of love, hope, trust, and enthusiasm of the Spirit, are not going to be entirely verified by such a restrictive method. And if one confines God to an objective being within the universe, that reality is not going to be found scientifically. Physicists even struggled to find an objectively real irreducible particle let alone a reality that is not an object. Religious people do not postulate that God can be confined to cosmology.

Science and religion do not need to spar with each other. Science can continue to discover and explain verifiable facts about the universe, and religion can make use of philosophical and theological concepts to give our existence purpose and meaning. The Biblical myth of the creation does not need to be viewed as scientific or historical fact, but can be interpreted as a story attributing our origins ultimately to God. And religion does not have to create dogma out of scientific observations that later need to be rescinded.

In some ways both science and religion have verifiable invisible energy fields that pervade our universe. Scientists concentrate on electrons and protons in this research, while religious persons experience what they describe as Spirit impacting their lives.

Scientists and mystics often have similar experiences. When they each reduce everything down to nothingness, both have an intense appreciation of Mystery. What can't be seen or described exists. Within this nothingness the ultimate Source of life is experienced in a mystical fashion.

'Giving It to Them'

Many years ago as I greeted people following a Sunday morning service, one parishioner said to me, "You really gave it to them, preacher." He didn't say, "Your sermon was meaningful to me." For him, what I said seemed to apply only to the others in the congregation, giving him a little lift in self-righteousness. I don't remember what the sermon was about, but I haven't forgotten that sometimes what we hear is used as evidence against others rather than applying the message to ourselves. I trust my intention was not to be in anyone's face, but that is a reaction I got.

When we see something wrong in the world or in another person, it is easy to pull the self-righteousness stop by condemning the offender and patting ourselves on the back. Jesus was familiar with this attitude and warned his hearers about exalting themselves at the expense of others. In the parable of the Pharisee and the tax collector who went up to the temple to pray, the Pharisee extolled himself as one who was not a thief, rogue, adulterer, or even like the tax collector. "But the tax collector, standing far off, would not even look up to heaven, but was beating his breast and saying, 'God, be merciful to me, a sinner!'" Jesus went on to say that "this man went down to his home justified rather than the other; for all who exalt themselves will be humbled, but all who humble themselves will be exalted. (Luke 18:9-14)

Like the Pharisee, enthusiastic evangelists sometimes fall into this accusatory trap. Instead of proclaiming "good news" with humility, there can be an "in your face" approach to the proclamation that turns off the audience and only makes the preacher feel good that he really "gave it to them." My experience many years ago is a warning to keep myself in the company of sinners. In being compassionate to myself I am more likely to be compassionate to others.

'Come Dance with Me'

The Sufi master, Hafiz (1320-1389), is the most beloved poet of Persia. When he died he was thought to have written an estimated 5,000 poems, of which 500 to 700 have survived. In one of these poems he wrote that God only knows four words. Here is the poem:

Every child has known God,
Not the God of names,
Not the God of don'ts
Not the God who ever does anything weird,
But the God who only knows four words
And keeps repeating them, saying:
"Come dance with Me."
Come dance.

Poets have license to express themselves any way they like to make a point. Certainly Hafiz has reminded us that our life with God is meant to be a dance, a relationship of joy. The Psalmist wrote, "Let them praise his Name in the dance; let them sing praise to him with timbrel and harp." (Psalm 149:3) When David led the Ark of the Covenant to Jerusalem, he danced before the Lord (2 Samuel 6:14). And in the New Testament dance is a natural part of the celebration of the return of the prodigal son (Luke 15:25).

The movement in dance expresses the whole person – body, mind, and spirit, and has found its place in celebrations and worship. It also expresses the relationship we are meant to have with God – one that activates our whole being, embraced in fluid affection in response to wonder and joy. The do's and don'ts of law and tradition are not meant to stifle exuberant love.

We are invited to accept God's invitation:

"Come dance with Me."

Swords into Plowshares

Among the prophecies looking toward a glorious future for Israel and the restoration of the Davidic kingdom is the hope for peace whereby weapons of war will be turned into instruments of peace. The people "shall beat their swords into plowshares, and their spears into pruning hooks; nation shall not lift up sword against nation, neither shall they learn war any more." (Isaiah 2:4; Micah 4:3-4)

Moving from a time of war to a time of peace is everyone's hope. Yet, nations perpetually prepare and engage in war. In recent years the United States has been involved in two wars. According to the Center for Arms Control and Non-Proliferation nearly half of all our taxes go to support the military. America not only spends more money on the military than any other nation, but more than all other nations combined. It is curious that a nation still claiming to be Christian spends more money on "swords" and "spears" than "plowshares." The consequence is that war machinery robs the poor and the hopes of our children.

In an attempt to support our troops we tend to worship the god of Mars rather than the God of Peace. Some military leaders, however, have been loath to do that, notably Dwight D. Eisenhower. Eisenhower was not an anti-war radical but a five star general and President of the United States. In 1953 he wrote about this dilemma:

"Every gun that is made, every warship launched, every rocket fired, signifies, in the final sense, a theft from those who are hungry and are not fed, those who are cold and are not clothed. The world in arms is not spending money alone. It is spending the sweat of its laborers, the genius of its scientists, the hopes of its children…This is not the way of life at all, in any true sense. Under the cloud of threatening war, it is humanity hanging on a cross of iron." (*A Book of Wonders*, E. Hays)

This statement reflects the attitude of Jesus. When he was arrested and his life threatened with crucifixion, Jesus' response to one who took a sword, striking the slave of the high priest and cutting off his ear, was, "Put your sword back into its place; for all who take the sword will perish by the sword." (Matt. 26:52)

Endless preparations for war, intended for peace, usually lead to war. Jesus' observation is too often true. And with atomic weapons that can exterminate humanity, the pacifist's approach may be the most practical. "Put your sword back into its place." Turn your "swords" into "plowshares."

Visiting the Graveyard

Last month our nation observed Memorial Day, a time to remember those who gave their lives in the service of our country. Perhaps on that day you visited the grave of one killed in action, or the burial plot of a beloved family member. Maybe you just strolled through the cemetery thinking about those who had lived and are now at rest. You noticed the setting, observed the beauty, and placed a flower on a stone.

Mary Oliver conveys in poetry this experience.
When I think of death
it is a bright enough city,
and every year more faces there
are familiar
but not a single one

notices me,
though I long for it,
and when they talk together,
which they do
very quietly,
it's in an unknowable language –
I can catch the tone
But understand not a single word –
And when I open my eyes
There's the mysterious field, the beautiful trees.
There are the stones.

I have officiated at numerous burial services and have spent personal time reflecting on the lives of my family whose graves date back to the late 18th Century. Many generations of my family are buried in the same cemetery. Whether I am participating in the burial of a recently departed person or reflecting on the lives of the departed in a meditative walk, something within me seems to say, "It is okay." It's a blessed gift that these people lived and are now at rest. It seems particularly okay and comforting to remember those who lived their lives in the Lord and who have died in the Lord. In the words of a burial service, "For none of us has life in himself, and none becomes his own master when he dies. For if we have life, we are alive in the Lord, and if we die, we die in the Lord. So, then, whether we live or die, we are the Lord's possession. Happy from now on are those who die in the Lord! So it is, says the Spirit, for they rest from their labors."

At the time of a death we feel grief and loss. But in periods of reflection we can remember that we are part of a bigger picture. We are part of the Mystery of God both in life and in death. So whether we live or die, we are the Lord's possession.

Graduation

In the month of May graduation ceremonies are celebrated throughout the country. Colleges and schools observed the completion of students' studies with good wishes for future learning and success in life. With three granddaughters graduating, I enjoyed participating in these memorable moments of passage.

At one of these graduation exercises the valedictorian, Emily, commented that there was a hum in the air, "a subtle melody composed of the energy of our wishes, our hopes – our future. We are so tightly coiled tonight, so ready to spring out in the world. Who will we be? What will we do? Here, in this slice of green in a grey city, our buzzing thoughts can mingle with the buzzing atmosphere. I see all this natural beauty, and I think – the trees, the stars – tonight I almost envy them. A tree's goal in life, their 'future,' is very simple: to go on indefinitely in their tree-ness. They do not angst and worry. A tree never bites its fingernails. And it is never so happy as when it is being truly, deeply, itself." She went on to say, however, that we as lumbering sentient beings put all sorts of rules and regulations on our abilities and say, "We must do this – we must go here – we must enjoy that. We run in all directions, we prowl cities and dorm rooms and self-help books and cry, 'What are we going to be in this life?' When in reality, we don't have to be anything. We already are. We are humans."

Her fine address reminded me that many look forward to the day when they will be someone. This usually means that one must achieve success admired by others. Our personal worth is thus determined by what others think of us – not in who we are. Yet, the gift of life given to us automatically makes us important beings, created in the image of the great Mystery. The challenge is to become fully human, embracing our spiritual and earthly natures to discover what it means to be whole and healthy human beings. Unlike a tree, we do have to reflect on values for our lives, but innate worth has already been given to us by God. That is cause for celebration whether or not we achieve public accolades.

Graduation for us is a willingness to discover and enjoy the gifts of beauty, the "atoms that nestle in the fabric of our graduation gowns that wriggle with the expectation of evening festivities. Our inner humanness, our deepest root is love and joy, and if we think that our jobs or college choices are somehow our true self, we have made mundane the beauty of our own humanity. All we're meant to do is to run out in the middle of a thunderstorm and scream with the pure raw delight of being alive. All we're meant to do is to hold out a hand to our fellow humans and say, 'Come dance with me.'"

'Those Little White Lies'

Some readers may remember a popular song many years ago called, "Those Little White Lies."
The moon was all aglow,
and heaven was in your eyes
the night that you told me
those little white lies.
The stars all seemed to know
that you didn't mean all those sighs;
the night that you told me
those little white lies.
I try, but there's no forgetting;
when evening appears,
I sigh, but there's no regretting,
in spite of my tears.
The devil was in your heart,
but heaven was in your eyes;
the night that you told me
those little white lies.
Who wouldn't believe those lips;
who ever could doubt those eyes;

71

the night that you told me,
those little white lies.

While it might seem unlikely that this song and a passage from Ephesians have something in common, both address relationships and telling the truth. Rather than having the devil in one's heart, as the song mentions, the Epistle admonishes us to speak the truth in love. (Ephesians 4:1-7, 11-16) We are to grow up in every way into Christ with humility, gentleness and patience, bearing with one another in love.

The admonition to "speak the truth in love" may seem obvious needing no further consideration. But my experience with people in their relationships indicates that while blatant lies are discouraged, little white lies are customary to avoid unpleasantness. Problems arise, however, when dishonesty in little things breaks trust and leads to dishonesty in big things. That is one of those clichés that remains true.

A long time ago I spoke with a couple before their marriage about the problems that little white lies can create. I told them an imaginary scene of a husband whose old flame came to town and wanted to meet with him just to say hello and have a drink. The husband wanted this too. But fearing that his wife might be jealous if he told her he was having a drink with his old girl friend, he told his wife that he had to work late at the office that evening and would be home late for dinner. That little white lie would allow him to see his friend without alarming his wife. What he didn't anticipate, however, was that one of his wife's friends would see him with his old girl friend at a cocktail lounge. The wife's friend suspected the worst, thinking that the husband was cheating on his marriage fidelity, and subsequently reported the incident to the wife. You can imagine the rest. The husband gets into trouble with his wife trying to explain his way out of what appears to be a cover-up for an illicit relationship.

After telling my made up story, the couple looked at each other almost embarrassed because that scenario had already happened to them while dating. They knew the point from first hand experience.

When we modify the truth in human relationships it leads to distrust and separation. Many relationships have been broken because the truth, even when told, couldn't be believed because of previous white lies.

Truth telling requires at least three things: knowing the truth, telling the truth, and telling it in a kind way, or at least in a way that the message can be received. It is also a matter of being honest with ourselves. Sometimes the problem is not so much about telling someone else the truth; it is a matter of being honest with ourselves and God. We tell ourselves little white lies and hope that God can be fooled in the same way.

Telling the truth is one part of the equation. Another part is telling it in love. One can tell the truth in such an abrasive way that the presentation is cruel. That is where the call for gentleness, patience, and bearing with one another is so important. Except for extreme situations we don't have to badger each other with the truth – nor be so zealous for our cause that we abuse others. We are admonished to maintain the unity of the Spirit in the bond of peace.

Vote for Jesus

There are yard signs around the County with the words, "Vote for Jesus." Since Jesus isn't running for any elective office, I am assuming that the signs are invitations to follow Jesus in one's life. Using the initials WWJD, "What would Jesus do," this slogan makes one wonder what Jesus would do if he were seeking an elected public office. At first glance that might seem like a good idea, but in reality the chances of Jesus being endorsed by a political party are nil.

Ray Waddle, a religion columnist, posed the question, "What if Jesus were on the presidential ballot?" Reflecting on the teachings of Jesus he noted that Jesus warned against ostentatious religious practice. "He sided against praying in public. He wasn't impressed with wealth: the big money is hostile to his gospel message. He said his followers should not pursue power. They should love their neighbor – even love their enemies – not lobby for the death penalty. If they love Jesus himself, they better love all people, even those on the margins, the failures, the sick, the repugnant." (The Tennessean, June 2, 2012)

Among Jesus' teachings preventing him from being a viable candidate for political office was his support of people sharing everything in common. He wasn't a communist as we know it, but he certainly wasn't a capitalist. Perhaps he would have been a socialist seeking the welfare of all people rather than encouraging competition that strives to get ahead of others for personal advantage.

When it comes to taxes, Jesus left that issue open ended. Taking a coin with the emperor's image, he said to give to the emperor the things that are the emperor's and to God the things that are God's. The moral of the story is that everything belongs to God. (Mark 12:13-17) Jesus would certainly not endorse half of U.S. taxes designated for war machinery. As noted, Jesus said, "Love your enemies and pray for those who persecute you." (Matt. 5:43-45)

Politicians can be fooled into thinking that Jesus would endorse their economic and political agendas simply because they go to church. Identifying WWJD with politically conservative evangelicals often doesn't match Jesus' teachings. As noted by Ray Waddell, "In the drama of daily spiritual decision, Jesus is always on the ballot, ever the long shot. For 2000 years running, his name again and again is manipulated, dishonored, crucified. Jesus isn't a political kingpin."

"Vote for Jesus" is a good reminder to reflect on his teachings and to examine our own prejudices, likes, and dislikes. Do our political and economic values uphold the inclusive unconditional love Jesus taught? Or is a vote for Jesus only an endorsement of one's personal point of view?

In the Name of God

When we pray God is usually addressed with a name and the intention of our prayer concluded with a similar expression. Christians might use one of the names of the Trinity: Father, Son, and Holy Spirit. Muslims traditionally begin prayer with "Allahu akbar" or "God is most great." Jews use a variety of expressions such as "Lord our God."

It is appropriate for all three religions to address their prayer to the God of Abraham since they all claim their origins come from Abraham. In a mixed gathering of religious people when specific titles for God might be divisive, one could sum up a prayer with the words, "In the Name of God."

"In the Name of God" is also used in a negative fashion with cursing. The intention of the cursing might not be to denigrate God but rather to let off steam when frustrated or angry. Religious people nevertheless consider this kind of profanity inappropriate.

Throughout history good works have been done in the Name of God such as the building of hospitals and schools and ministries to the poor and needy. Great violence has also been inflicted in the Name of God such as the killing of Muslims by Christians at the time of the Crusades, the execution of Catholics and Protestants by each other during the Reformation with beheadings and burnings at the stake, and in the promotion of prejudice in modern day settings. In the 1950's for example, Christians had a slogan, "Kill a Commie for Christ," as if Christ was opposed to all political and economic systems that didn't embrace democracy and capitalism. On racial issues I was told by a seminary professor of ethics that black people don't have souls like white people, thus leaving the option that black people don't have to be respected with the same love and justice due white people. Today religious bodies pass resolutions against homosexuals as if sexual orientation were a matter of choice rather than

God given as is our skin. "In the Name of God" can be acted upon as a blessing or a curse.

When we invoke the name of God it behooves us to examine our intentions. Do we pray for God's healing and blessing in the activities of our lives, or are we simply calling upon God to agree with our fears, prejudices, and hatreds?

Merton's Prayer

Thomas Merton was one of the greatest American spiritual masters of the 20th Century. He was born in Prades, in Southern France, in 1915. In 1941 he entered the Trappist Monastery at Gethsemani, Kentucky. He was a prolific author excelling in his understanding of the contemplative life of prayer. He died an untimely death while visiting Bangkok in December 1968.

Among his many writings is a beautiful prayer of dedication and trust. It is found in his book, *Thoughts in Solitude*. The prayer has had a profound influence on many who say the prayer in their devotions. At first it seems an unlikely prayer from a spiritual master who begins by saying, "My Lord God, I have no idea where I am going. I do not see the road ahead of me. I cannot know for certain where it will end." For those of us who admire Merton it is hard to imagine that with all his spiritual insight he would not know where he was going. Of all people he surely should know the way. But it is because he was so deeply in love with God that he could offer himself humbly in prayer trusting only that his desire to please God was in itself pleasing to God. His immense learning opened up windows to the Mystery of God rather than providing certainty with answers. Thus, he could pray that his only desire was to trust God always though he might seem to be lost and in the shadow of death. Perhaps this prayer will speak to your heart too and be an offering of your life to God in simple trust.

"My Lord God, I have no idea where I am going. I do not see the road ahead of me. I cannot know for certain where it will end. Nor do I really know myself, and the fact that I think that I am following your will does not mean that I am actually doing so. But I believe that the desire to please you does in fact please you. And I hope I have that desire in all that I am doing. I hope that I will never do anything apart from that desire. And I know that if I do this you will lead me by the right road though I may know nothing about it. Therefore will I trust you always though I may seem to be lost and in the shadow of death. I will not fear, for you are ever with me, and you will never leave me to face my perils alone."

Beauty

Imagine it's summertime – a good time to lean back from the routine of our busy lives and to enjoy friends and family. It can be a time for refreshment and renewal too – a time to be open to the goodness of God in creation. Leisure time provides the opportunity to recall the many ways that God speaks through beauty – in creation, in persons, even in us.

If the pursuit of beauty is appealing to you in the summer, you may find that your appreciation of something beautiful may not be shared. As the saying goes, "Beauty is in the eye of the beholder." What is beautiful to one person may be ugly to another. Trash along the roadside is ugly to most of us; but trash, arranged in a modern art gallery, may be considered beautiful or at least art with a message. Dropping the lid of a grand piano may be a shocking, unpleasant noise; or it might be an integral part of a John Cage musical composition. Cage sought to break down the barrier between "art" and "non-art" maintaining that all sounds are of interest. One composition calls for 4 minutes and 33 seconds of silence – time when whatever sound is going on around the listener becomes part of the composition – a siren, a bird call, or a belch.

This approach to art and beauty makes one wonder where beauty can or cannot be found. In religious circles there is often an attempt to distinguish between the sacred and the profane – the things that enhance our appreciation of the holiness of God and those things that distract us. For some the difference between the sacred and profane is significant. But for others, holiness and the beauty of God can be found in all things, even in things considered ugly or imperfect.

The Celtic tradition that dominated Great Britain and Ireland from the third century into the ninth minimizes distinctions between the sacred and profane. Its legacy sees creation as essentially good. And the role of the Church is not to be a custodian of salvation, dispensing salvation according to restrictive rules of a hierarchical institution, but rather as a liberator to give access to the treasure of God's goodness that is at the very heart of all life. It is available even in the ordinariness of our lives. Any time is a good time to touch, feel, and taste the presence of God in love relationships and in creation, even in things considered ugly.

Redemption is about being reconnected to the beauty that has been planted at the heart of all being. The challenge for us is to accept our true identity – to be brought back to a place of beauty – to the God who dwells within us. As Jesus said, "The kingdom is within you."

Acceptance of this gift is critical to the acceptance of others. By receiving it for ourselves we are more likely to see good in others. Without that awareness, instead of seeing beauty in others, we tend to focus on their flaws. Somehow we need to remember that we were created in beauty…that God dwells in us…that Love is luring us to hear the "heartbeat of God." It is the beat of Beauty without which nothing that is would be."

As you take leisure time this summer, I hope that you will find refreshment for your souls by reawakening the heartbeat of God in your life. Become as if a child again and enjoy the delicate form and color of a flower. When you walk through a field, don't fail to notice the color purple. Open yourself to a new awareness of the beauty of God in all things, even in those things covered by a disguise.

Bloom Where You Are Planted

A popular poster years ago read, "Bloom where you are planted." It is a phrase encouraging us to take a positive approach to life in whatever circumstances we find ourselves.

Taking this advice is easier for some than others. While there is so much in life to enjoy, we recognize at the same time that pain and frustration are frequent. This presents us with a choice – to succumb to a negative attitude and multiply its sorrow with our disappointments, or to move forward by planting a seed in the soil given to us – to bring forth some fruit of joy.

One who modeled this for us was Jesus. He was planted on the soils of a poor country. For the most part his circumstances were ordinary and insignificant. His birth was humble, his livelihood simple, his ministry short-lived and in a small area. He didn't win a Rotary prize. He died as a criminal and was deserted by his friends. Who would imagine that a man born to be king would die as a crook; and who would imagine that kings and heroes of the past are now forgotten but the Jesus of Nazareth lives, shaping the course of our lives.

The circumstances of our lives are often not as important as what we do with the given-ness of our situations. People like Helen Keller (1880-1968), who lost her hearing and sight when she was 19 months old from an illness, led an inspirational life. She earned a college degree and became a prolific author and political activist, campaigning for women's suffrage and labor rights.

Jesus, with unfavorable circumstances, exercised the same stamina. Even with a life cut short he didn't lose the debate that love eventually conquers evil. Love may be flogged and nailed to a cross, but a new twig appears insisting on beauty. That is the gift given to each of us if we choose to blossom where we are planted.

God Said What?!

There are times when we might wish that the Bible had definitive answers for every issue affecting our lives. Wouldn't it be nice to have an inerrant answer book that could give us absolute certainty about God and the way we are meant to treat each other? Of course, if that were true we wouldn't have to have faith, which is the opposite of certitude. And God would no longer be the great Mystery. We would have finally captured God and brought God down to our level.

The Bible was not dropped from heaven in the Authorized King James Version as revered by some. The Bible is an ancient record of people's experience with God. It shows a developing understanding of who God is. At first people thought there were many gods, but only one for Israel. Later they came to see that there is only one God for all people. To preserve the oral tradition of their experiences and stories for future generations, scribes recorded this heritage with its history and myths. The authors of the New Testament did the same, desiring to preserve the memory of Jesus. It wasn't until the fourth century that the Church decided which of the many writings available should be authorized as sacred texts. This was determined by vote, including hostility and the banishing of some writings rediscovered in the 1940's. The Book of Revelation and Ecclesiastes, for example, barely made it into the collection. Even today all churches in Christendom don't include the same texts.

While we might wish that we had the verbatim words of God recorded in scripture, we can be grateful that we don't, or we would have to worship a God who is in favor of genocide, slavery, subservience of women, and the stoning of disobedient children. These are a few of the directives supposedly spoken by God. When Saul conquered the Amalekites he failed to kill all of their animals, women and children, a command Samuel said was the will of God. So

Samuel completed the destruction of the Amalekite people
with his own hands. (1 Samuel 15) In the New Testament,
according to Ephesians 6:5, it is said that slaves are to obey
their earthly masters, leaving the assumption that slavery is
acceptable to God. Women in the Old Testament were
regarded as property, and in the New Testament wives must
continue to accept the authority of their husbands. (1 Peter
3:1) In Deuteronomy we hear that if a child disobeys his
parents the "men of the town shall stone him to death."
(Deut. 21:18-21) If directives like these are to be considered
words from God, one might ask, "God said what?!" Such
requirements hardly match the God of love we experience in
our lives.

Ascribing words to God is often misleading. Not until
recent times has the Bible been considered a literal, inerrant
summary of God's words. Rather, the Bible is the foundation
for a continuing revelation of God to us. Jesus himself moved
us forward into a deeper understanding of love that surpasses
law, and the Holy Spirit still has a lot to teach us about the
compassionate God that brought us into existence. What
God may be saying to us may only be heard in the secrets of
our hearts.

Love Stories

There are many love stories in the Bible. Isaac's love for
Rebecca may be the first to come to mind. He was sent forth
by his father Abraham to find a wife. Rebecca appears and
draws water for him and his camels. After receiving
permission from Rebecca's father and brother, this arranged
marriage is greeted with Rebecca's consent. They go on to
have twin boys, Jacob and Esau.

Jacob and Rachel's relationship was not so easy. Jacob saw
a shepherdess at a well. Her name was Rachel. Jacob fell in
love with her and promised to work seven years for her father
Laban in order to receive his permission to marry Rachel. As
it happened, Laban tricked Jacob into marrying Leah,

Rachel's elder sister. So Jacob had to work another seven years in order to make Rachel his bride. In Hebrew Bible days, men could have more than one wife. King David had at least eight wives who are named, and his son, Solomon, had 700 wives and 300 concubines. Our preference these days in the western world is to have one wife at a time.

Thinking of David, there is his scandalous love affair with Bathsheba. David saw Bathsheba bathing on a rooftop and gave in to his temptation. When she became pregnant David had to think of a way to get rid of her husband, Uriah. So he ordered Uriah into the front lines of battle where he was killed. David was then free to marry Bathsheba. Although they lost their first child, Bathsheba was the mother of Solomon through whom Jesus' lineage to King David is traced.

A love story that is sometimes overlooked is David and Jonathan's deep love for each other. The traditional interpretation has them forming a political covenant and a close, non-sexual friendship. We read in Second Samuel David's great distress at the death of Jonathan, whom he calls his brother. "Greatly beloved were you to me," he says. "Your love to me was wonderful, passing the love of women."

Some scholars today believe that Jonathan and David were lovers based on the way the story is presented and on the Hebrew words used to describe their relationship. The actual nature of their relationship may continue to entertain speculation, but their love for each other is not in question. It is another of the rich love stories of the Bible.

These love stories uphold the deepest message of the Bible. The Bible is ultimately the story of love. In both the old and new testaments we learn that we are to love God and our neighbor as ourselves. Paul upheld this virtue when he wrote that the greatest gift is love, surpassing faith and hope.

In our personal lives most of us have discovered that love is what gives our lives meaning and joy. In the intimacy of relationships we get a glimpse of the deep love that God has for each of us. Intimacy with God is often learned through intimacy with another person. It can be the most cherished gift in a marriage or committed relationship.

The greatest love story of all, of course, is God's love for us expressed in the life, death, and resurrection of Jesus. "For God so loved the world that he gave his only Son, so that everyone who believes in him may not perish but may have eternal life." It is no wonder that John 3:16 and succeeding verses have become a beloved passage of scripture. The story is not about God's desire to torture us in hell, but to love us in all things and to grant us the joy of discovering what love can mean in our relationships with one another. God cherishes our love stories and seeks to embrace us every moment of our lives.

Words or Word

A world of words! We speak them, read them, write and sing them. Words express our thoughts and emotions. Poets paint pictures for our imaginations. Stories and lies can be told – curses and comfort conveyed.

Since words are symbols of our thoughts, we need to say what we mean. "A rose is a rose is a rose is a rose" may have been true for Gertrude Stein, but for most of us a rose can be red, white, or yellow, hybrid or antique. (From "Sacred Emily," 1913) The picture of a rose that comes to each of us may be different. The words we choose may or may not convey what we mean.

Words are constantly being invented. When I was a child my family referred to teasing as "kidology." My spell check says that's not a word, but it worked for us.

"Supercalifragilisticexpialidocious" wasn't a real word when it was first used in the musical Mary Poppins, but spell check says it's okay now.

Words have always been important, and today we continue that pursuit by being politically sensitive to others by our choice of words and the issues we discuss. That is especially true when we speak of the ethnic and racial origins of people. We try to avoid words that denigrate a person's dignity. We may also avoid words that raise "red flags" – words and issues that are so "hot" that an emotional response clouds objective thinking.

We are sensitive to language and images in the church as well. While we are not afraid to deal with controversial issues, and take risks to know the Truth, our choice of words is governed by what seems appropriate for any given congregation. We especially strive to use words that convey what we mean to say about God. For example, we are accustomed to praying, "In the name of the Father, and of the Son, and of the Holy Spirit." That phrase is the traditional way to express the doctrine of the Trinity – God in three persons, yet one God. For some people, however, the word "Father" confines God to male gender. Since God is beyond the limitations of gender, God might also be called "Mother." We don't choose to call God "It" because that would imply that God is a thing that doesn't understand the emotions of human beings. Trying not to limit God to a male or female role is a challenge for preachers. All of a sudden there are no pronouns that one can use for God. So if the word "God" appears several times in the course of a sentence, one chooses another name for God that is appropriate, such as Creator – or in the case of the Son, Redeemer, and the Holy Spirit as Giver of Life. The Holy Spirit is sometimes given a feminine image as well.

Perhaps the most important choice of words comes in the translation of ancient biblical texts into modern languages. Scholarship has brought clarity to new translations. Old translations said we were to forgive "seventy times seven" on any given occasion. More recent translations read that one should forgive "seventy-seven" times. Do we forgive 77 times or 490 times before lambasting our adversaries? The Greek number can be legitimately understood as "seventy seven times" as in Gen. 4:24. Jesus' statement is a reversal of Lamech's pronouncement of vengeance. Lamech, a descendant of Cain, said to his wives: "Adah and Zillah, hear my voice; you wives of Lamech, listen to what I say: I have killed a man for wounding me, a young man for striking me. If Cain is avenged sevenfold, truly Lamech seventy-sevenfold." Jesus' point is that instead of vengeance one should offer forgiveness. The number of times is not a matter of math or linguistics, but of the nature of forgiveness.

One controversial word in biblical translations that does make a difference in the way we read and understand a passage of Scripture is the word "homosexual." In the Revised Standard Version of the Bible, Paul's long list of wrongdoers who will not inherit the kingdom of God includes "homosexuals" as well as unbelieving civil judges. The New Revised Standard Version of the Bible uses the words "male prostitutes," however, rather than homosexuals, not only to be more accurate to what Paul was trying to convey, but also because in those days there was little understanding of the genetic and psychological makeup of people with a homosexual orientation. (First Corinthians 6:9)

Language changes can be troublesome. Unfortunately, there are those whose faith is attached to certain words, so that when the word is changed, so is their faith.

What, then, do words have to do with our religious life?

"In the beginning was the Word, and the Word was with God, and the Word was God." (John 1:1) Those are the opening words of the Gospel of John, where the author sees Jesus as the "logos" of God – Word that is more than speech. It is God in action, creating (Gen. 1:3; Ps. 33:6), revealing (Am. 3:7-8), redeeming (Ps. 107:19-20). (NRSV Commentary) Such a passage reminds us that living into the Word is not a matter of words, but of a living relationship with God who is creating, revealing, and redeeming. One of our tendencies in religion is to try to get it right. We want to tack down everything we know about God, turn it into doctrines, dogmas, and creeds, and then to insist that everyone live by those formularies. That practice is perfectly understandable since people often prefer certitude to faith. They would rather think they have God figured out than to live into the unknown mystery of God, into a relationship of vulnerability, intimacy, and trust. Those latter qualities, of course, are essential for any relationship of love. One can attempt to follow a textbook on marriage, for example, but if a couple is not willing to be vulnerable to one another, to grow into the unknown together, to grant one another trust and unconditional love, the marriage won't achieve the high qualities for which it was designed. Obeying the letter of the law in the words of the Bible won't guarantee a loving relationship with God and with our fellow human beings either. Any attempt to capture God through words and a collection of books is as dangerous as molding a golden calf. In the Christian experience, words are tools of communication to tell the story of freedom and God's love for us, and through that story to bring us into a relationship of love with God and one another.

The divisions we cause ourselves by organizing opposing camps based on proof texts from Scripture need to be broken down by seeing the bigger picture of the Word of God in action – creating, revealing, and redeeming – an action designed to reconcile us all to God in one body.

May the words we use, even in their imperfection, tell the story of God's love, and lead us into the joy of the greatest mystery of all, the Word.

Kindness

Some of us may benefit from a refresher course in kindergarten. Kindergarten (from the Old High German kinder, the plural of kind, child) as described by Edward Hays "was originally designed as an orientation adjustment from home to school for children ages four to five." It was a place where children could learn to interact with one another and learn kindness. Practicing kindness would teach them polite behavior, courteous respect for one another, and how to express gratitude for simple acts of service. This we expect from our children when kindness is practiced in a home. In advanced years, however, many are not as concerned about being kind as they are advancing their self-interest even if it means putting other people down. Bullying is even upheld as political patriotism.

St. Paul on the other hand encouraged his readers to be kind. Kindness is one of the fruits of the Spirit. (Galatians 5:22-23) As we know, it is sometimes hard to be kind when we are mistreated. Our initial instinct might be to fight back. But Paul taught not to return evil for evil, but goodness. (1 Thessalonians 5:15) He understood Jesus' compassionate approach to "do good to those who hate you, bless those who curse you, pray for those who abuse you. (Luke 6:27-28) Jesus understood the weakness in others. His motive was not to get even with those who offended him but to provide an alternative – a loving heart.

Kindness includes a thoughtful relationship towards others providing help and assurance when it is needed. While we might think that the recipients of our kindness are those closest to us, we sometimes forget to be kind since they are the ones most likely to forgive us for rude remarks. Teasing can also be an issue. Teasing is not always funny. Teasing can be hurtful when we disguise criticism with humor. After the laugh there may be a tear.

Whether we choose to take a refresher course in kindergarten or not, remembering to be kind is the behavior that exemplifies the work of the Spirit. There is enough evil in this world without adding fuel to the fire. Love, joy, peace, patience, kindness, generosity, faithfulness, gentleness, and self-control are more likely to bring us into harmony with one another and the Spirit.

A Broken Heart

While we often marvel at the beauty of creation, tragedy and sorrow are also a part of our experience. We wonder how a good God can allow horrible events to happen, such as genocides and injustice, and why in nature we cannot control earthquakes, drought, and hurricanes that produce death, famine, and disease. Job tried to figure out this dilemma. Elie Wiesel dramatized the problem in his play, *The Trial of God*, presenting the horrors of Jewish holocausts. But even with our excuses given for God to allow these losses, we can only come up with ways to deal with them. If we were God we wouldn't allow evil to exist.

We are not God, of course, and have to deal with many broken hearts. Fortunately, loving and compassionate natures bring healing to those who hurt; and on occasion great goodness arises from the trauma. Some have turned the pain of tragedy into an opportunity for new life.

The phoenix, a fabulous bird that periodically regenerated itself from the fire, has become a symbol of death and resurrection for many. When the phoenix reached the end of its life it burned itself on a pyre of flames, and from the ashes a new phoenix arose. And so it is for some who have experienced broken hearted events in their lives, but from the "ashes" new life and hope has arisen.

Mary Oliver in a poem tells the story of loons who came to her harbor and died, one by one. She writes, "A friend told me of one on the shore that lifted its head and opened the elegant beak and cried out in the long, sweet savoring of its life which, if you have heard it, you know is a sacred thing, and for which, if you have not heard it, you had better hurry to where they still sing. And, believe me, tell no one just where that is. The next morning this loon, speckled and iridescent and with a plan to fly home to some hidden lake, was dead on the shore. I tell you this to break your heart, by which I mean only that it break open and never close again to the rest of the world." (Poem Lead)

There are times when breaking open our hearts is just what God might wish us to do – to cry with God to express our mutual feelings of suffering and loss.

By example, a young peacemaker, John Leary (1958-1982), while pursuing his degree from Harvard College, devoted the last six years of his life to ministry with prisoners, the homeless, and the elderly. He engaged in protests over the military draft, capital punishment, and abortion regarding all such issues to be joined in a "seamless garment" approach to the defense of human life. He kept his broken heart open to minister to the needs of those who suffer and who would minimize the beauty of human life. He died at the age of twenty-four from a heart attack while running.

Leary's broken heart can be a reminder to us to engage in ministry to those in need and not to turn away from the pain around us. We cannot solve all problems, but we can at least bring healing to those who suffer because of human neglect. A broken heart may be all we need to get started.

Silence

At times it is hard to hear the sound of silence. With smart phones humming, conversations babbling, music, news, and commercials commanding our attention, our days can be filled with noise. For some these sounds are companions, even to keeping the television on all night while sleeping. Yet, non-stop exterior sound can distract one from listening to the inner silent sounds of the Spirit wishing to be heard. God's first language, after all, is silence, and without that silence we may miss what God seeks to say to us in the depths of our hearts.

Silence is usually understood as the absence of any sound or noise that the ear might hear. But silence can include silence of the mind and the will as well. Refraining from talk or listening to music may be hard for some, but quieting the mental noise of memory and imagination is much harder. As some have discovered, the "hardest of all is to still the voices of craving and aversion within the will."

All the miraculous resources of our technological age seem to conspire to keep our ears, minds, and wills perpetually engaged. It can become a collaboration of distraction hindering us from perceiving the intuitions of the Spirit.

Turning off sound and letting go of any thought can begin to quiet the mind.

To help with this exercise there is a prayer form known as Centering Prayer that many practice to quiet the imagination, feelings, and rational faculties in order to be engaged with God in pure faith in silence. This contemplative prayer provides a point of communing with God beyond the limitations of words, thoughts, and actions. One simply sits quietly in the presence of God to offer God quality time. This provides an opportunity for the Spirit to pray within us, especially when we don't know how to pray.

Some have discovered the need to designate time each day to go into their room and shut the door and to be silent before God (Matt. 6:6). In this time one turns off the bombardment of advertising that intensifies our cravings, technical devices that scream for our attention, and the cacophony of audible sounds that keep us perpetually distracted. It is simply a time to be with God – no formal prayers or readings, no attachment to any thought, just a time to let go of everything and to be naked before God. God is often found in the nothingness when we cease to be busy looking for God.

The Psalmist was wise when he wrote, "For God alone my soul in silence waits; from him comes my salvation. Truly, my hope is in him." (Psalm 62: 1, 6)

Mend or Mangle

When someone upsets you there are at least two options for a response. You can strike back by giving the attacker a "piece of your mind," or you can let the blow stop with you. Hurtful remarks returned with equal vehemence perpetuate the problem and can lead to mangled relationships. The alternative is let the anger stop with you, returning evil with good. (Luke 6:27-38)

In personal relationships we know that Jesus' admonition to love our enemies and to forgive those who hurt us is a way to bring healing. Goodness ultimately has greater appeal than violence. But ever since 1945 when the United States dropped the big bombs over Japan we know that we or any other nuclear power has the potential to destroy all living creatures. Being fearful that someone will drop bombs on us we proceed to develop greater military superiority to discourage such an attack or at least to be equipped to administer devastating retaliation.

In 1958 the Nobel Peace Prize recipient, Dominique Georges Pire, said: "If an atomic bomb falls on the world tomorrow, it is because I argued with my neighbor today." Edward Hays remarks, "That insightful comment reveals how the chain of events you initiate can have a profound impact on the world. But the chain can work for good as well. Instead of giving someone "a piece of your mind," you can give them "the peace of your mind."

The song, "Let there be peace on earth," is a good reminder that peace on earth should begin with each one of us. The dance of evil doesn't have to be repeated with vengeance against the attacker. That response can set off a chain reaction of destruction leading to annihilation. Some countries, for example, stay in conflict with one another generation after generation. Children are taught to hate the enemy. On occasion they don't even know the reason why. And thus, they risk becoming friends. This is the sensitive message of the movie, "The Boy in the Striped Pajamas," where a German Arian boy befriends a Jewish child. They find no reason to hate each other but share the same fate.

Mending relationships with peace instead of a "piece of one's mind" is the loving and healing approach. It is also the safest.

'Jesus...have mercy on me'

Blind Bartimaeus shouted out into the crowd, "Jesus, Son of David, have mercy on me!" (Mark 10:47)

This cry of Bartimaeus for mercy and healing is a prayer that Christians through the centuries have used to ask for God's nearer presence in their lives. It is often referred to as the Jesus Prayer. Variations of the prayer include, "Lord Jesus Christ, Son of God, have mercy on me a sinner." Another phrase used to invite God's healing presence into one's life is the Aramaic word "maranatha" which means, Come Lord. Come Lord Jesus.

Some people use a phrase like this throughout the day as a mantra, repeating it many times so that it becomes a part of one's being. Rather than praying many words, one uses some short phrase or breath prayer to focus one's intention to live each day in the presence of God. The prayer is not meant to be a distraction but an act of self-dedication asking that our hearts, our minds and imaginations may be drawn closer to God.

In the Scriptures there are various pleas that have been used by people seeking God's nearer presence. For Bartimaeus it was a specific plea that he might receive his sight. For us it is often a plea that God's healing gifts will be granted to those who suffer in body, mind, or spirit, or that we might be healed of our own spiritual blindness. But beyond specific intentions, our prayer can be a simple offering of ourselves to God, trusting that God will do for us better things than we can imagine. It is a prayer that God's will be done in our lives.

When I use a word, or a breath prayer, or the Jesus prayer in my own practice, I am often not focusing on the words I say but on the intent of my heart to be present for God – to be healed of the ghosts of the past and to let the Spirit pray in me when I don't know how to pray. Paul speaks of this in the Letter to the Romans where he writes, "Likewise the Spirit helps us in our weakness; for we do not know how to pray as we ought, but that very Spirit intercedes with sighs too deep for words." (Rom 8:26) "Jesus, Son of David, have mercy on me" can very easily be this kind of prayer – one that doesn't try to take control of a situation in order to manipulate an outcome, but rather asks that God's mercy may surround us with healing grace and work in us those things that need to be accomplished.

Much of our journey into God arises spontaneously without the help of intellectual processes. We receive intuitions of truth. Simple words or a momentary thought can acknowledge these insights. We don't have to do anything with them, necessarily. Our response can simply be a little interior word "surging up from the depths of our spirit, the expression of one's whole being." (*The Cloud of Unknowing*) And this little word, bursting from the depths of one's spirit, may touch the heart of God more than some long prayer or discourse. That is not to discount liturgies that support community prayer; but a little word like "Help," or "My God," or "Jesus, Son of David, have mercy on me!" may be all that is required to turn us around to God's embrace.

What's on Your Mind?

After meeting a friend for a visit and settling into a conversation, you might ask, "What's on your mind?" It could be a general comment just to find out what the two of you might like to talk about, or it could be a slightly probing question to find out why your friend appears to have a frown on her face. Perhaps there is some issue she is dealing with. Perhaps as Mary Oliver writes in a poem, we can ask the question "as though it's some kind of weight." ("Four Sonnets")

And it might be a weight that needs to be lifted or at least shared to lighten the load. Simon of Cyrene did this in a literal sense by helping Jesus carry his cross up Calvary's hill. (Luke 23:26) But for us the help may be to lend a willing ear to listen as the weight of the problem is unraveled. A loving, unconditional acceptance of the one telling the story can be the beginning of healing as the problem is told. No instant cure or band-aid is expected – nor is appropriate. The healing most likely will not come from your advice but from within the one releasing the burden.

The solution to the problem revealed from the question, "What's on your mind?" needs to come from the one carrying the issue. Even if you think you know the solution, your job is to lighten the weight of the problem, to let your friend see it more clearly, and in the discernment to be with your friend as she puts it to rest.

Was Jesus Married?

Speculation regarding Jesus' marital status has been refreshed by the discovery of a Coptic papyrus fragment that scholars believe dates from the fourth century. From this fragment Jesus "appears to be in conversation about family and discipleship – Who is worthy? Who dwells with, and in, the Lord? The account contains a momentous line: 'Jesus said to them, 'My wife…'"

Through the centuries it has been assumed that Jesus was single since a wife is not mentioned in the canonical scriptures. But from other early writings we learn that Jesus was comfortable in the company of women and that he might have had a special relationship with Mary Magdalene. Scholars think it unlikely that Jesus and Mary Magdalene had a traditional Jewish marriage including a dowry from Mary's parents. Jesus and Mary were also free spirited in light of some of the remarks they made about family. But there is documentation as to the special nature of their relationship.

From early gospels not included in the Bible we learn that Mary Magdalene is the companion of Jesus and that they kissed each other often (Gospel of Philip 32). From the Gospel of Mary we read that Jesus loved her more than any other woman (6:1) and that Jesus knew her completely and loved her devotedly (10:10). There are also texts that support

Mary Magdalene being the Beloved Disciple rather than John. Some scholars offer the possibility that Mary Magdalene may even be the author of the Gospel of John. (Sandra M. Schneiders)

As my brother wrote in his last book, "The evidence is clear that Mary Magdalene and Jesus are companions, soul-mates, and partners in ministry." From his scholarly perspective all their work springs from their own experience with each other in a sacred union. He asks, "Is there any greater marriage than that?" (*Sacred Partnership* by John B. Butcher)

This new Coptic scrap of codex with the words, "Jesus said to them, 'My wife...'" came to the attention of Karen L. King of Harvard Divinity School by way of an anonymous collector. She says that this fragment is not evidence of Jesus' marital status, but taken together with the contemporaneous Gnostic gospels of Mary, Philip and Thomas, if in fact authentic, "does shed light on debates within early Christianity about sexuality and marriage." (Time 10/01/2012) In these debates celibacy was favored as a route to spiritual purity. While clergy were married in the early centuries of the Church, it was later discouraged and then prohibited by the Roman Catholic Church in 1139 at the Second Lateran Council. The assumption was that clergy were following the example of Jesus, observing sexual purity. A more practical reason for celibacy was that properties held by the Church and clergy did not have to be passed down to their legitimate children through inheritance.

It is noted that it would have been unusual for Jesus not to have been married. The expectation in the culture was that men would marry. We know, however, that St. Paul was not married and it is assumed that John the Baptist was single; but the first Pope, St. Peter, was married. His mother-in-law is mentioned in the Gospels (Mk. 1:30; Luke 4:38)

This contemporary discussion of whether or not Jesus had a wife opens up again the discussion of putting sexuality and marriage in a proper perspective. Most Christians have honored the union of marriage and have not given it a second place status as St. Paul did. Paul thought that if one's sexual urges were too strong, then one should be married (1 Cor. 7:09-36); but he suggested that if a spouse died, one should remain single awaiting the second coming of Christ assumed to be soon. A more common understanding as presented in "The Celebration and Blessing of a Marriage" in the Book of Common Prayer states that "The union of husband and wife in heart, body, and mind is intended by God for their mutual joy; for the help and comfort given one another in prosperity and adversity; and, when it is God's will, for the procreation of children and their nurture in the knowledge and love of the Lord." (BCP, p. 423)

The continuing discussion regarding Jesus' marital status is a titillating inquiry, but the outcome should it be verified one way or the other won't change our respect for those who marry and those who remain single. If anything, the possibility that Jesus was married only highlights his humanity as being one of us. And it is in his humanity that we have been able to see the divine light of God's presence in human form – a light that is intended to shine in each of us.

Welcome the Stranger

When visitors arrive at our churches or a new family moves into the neighborhood it is customary for us to be friendly and welcoming. It is especially easy to do when the newcomers seem to be people like ourselves. If they have a different ethnic or racial background, some may think twice about welcoming those who may or may not fit into the social structure of our community. This is particularly true when it comes to welcoming immigrants. Most of our families were immigrants sometime in the past, but we usually think of ourselves as the ones who have first priority on receiving the benefits of citizenship in the United States of America.

In recent years we have noted tension regarding Hispanics who have entered this country legally or illegally. Few condone the actions of those coming to this country illegally even if their reasons for coming are sound. Some states have gone to considerable trouble to block such entries or to deport those caught without the proper papers.

If one were to consider the Bible to be God's unerring word, it would be difficult to justify a hard-nosed approach to keeping the alien out. In Leviticus 23:22, God says, "When you reap the harvest of your land, you shall not reap to the very edges of your field, or gather the gleanings of your harvest; you shall leave them for the poor and for the alien: I am the Lord your God." In Leviticus 19:33-34 we read, "When an alien resides with you in your land, you shall not oppress the alien. The alien who resides with you shall be to you as the citizen among you; you shall love the alien as yourself, for you were aliens in the land of Egypt: I am the Lord your God."

There are all sorts of passages in the Bible that many of us do not consider the unerring word of God, but passages like these that commend us to welcome the stranger remind us that everyone is a child of God and that God encourages us to be compassionate in all circumstances. Our prejudices are not adequate permission to be hurtful to those who differ from us. Finding suitable solutions to immigration problems on a national level will undoubtedly continue to spark intense dialogue. But in our immediate relationships with aliens or strangers we are reminded to love them as ourselves, one of the two great commandments.

Christmas Is Hearing the Story

A member of my family asked me to write a song for her to be sung at her P.E.O. Christmas gathering. I suggested that she send me a poem to be set to music. To my happy surprise she wrote a Christmas poem that I would like to share with you.

'Til we hear the good news of the birth
and the star, is it Christmas?
Or just a merry December day?
Christmas is hearing the story.
'Til we sing Silent Night, Bethlehem, and
Noel, is it Christmas Eve?
Or just a busy December night?
Christmas is singing the story.
'Til we set out the crèche with its virgin
and babe, is it Christmas?
Is that tiny nativity first or last?
Christmas is seeing the story.
The baby, a couple, an angel, three
kings are the vision.
The carols and hymns, of peace and the
Son, are the song.
Luke Chapter Two, read from King
James, is the story.
Christmas is seeing
Christmas is singing
Christmas is hearing the story.
(Deborah W. Butcher)

Christmas is hearing the story that God chose to be part of human life in the person of Jesus. It is a continuing story telling us that we are not alone to fend for ourselves without God's love and presence. It is a story of Good News.

While Christmas is many things including shopping, gift giving, parties and greetings, it is especially a time for Christians to hear the story of Jesus' birth, to sing carols in his honor, and to see in crèches and decorations God's gift of love to us seen in a tiny babe. For those who have not heard the story it is especially good to tell. It is a story that can fill us with heaven's blessings.

Love Came Down at Christmas

One of the most cherished stories of this season is O. Henry's "The Gift of the Magi." It is the story of young Jim and Della. Newly wed and desperately poor, they nevertheless want to give each other an especially desired gift. Each is willing to sacrifice a particularly prized possession to do so: Jim, the gold watch that belonged to his Father; Della, her glorious cascade of hair. As it turns out, Jim buys Della beautiful combs, pure tortoise shell, with jeweled rims. But without her tresses the coveted combs lose their purpose and cannot be worn as an adornment. Della, as her gift, buys Jim a platinum fob chain, simple and chaste in design, properly proclaiming its value by substance alone. But without the watch, Jim's gift has no purpose and cannot be an adornment either.

The gifts Jim and Della chose cost more than either had bargained for, but in giving to each other, they received more than they had thought possible. It was their love that really counted, expressed in the generosity of their gifts to each other. Love, expressed through sacrifice, was the essence of their gifts. Although unwisely sacrificing the greatest treasurers of their house, these two were wise. As O. Henry (William Sydney Porter) writes, "Of all who give and receive gifts, such as they are wisest. Everywhere they are wisest. They are the magi."

At Christmas, when gifts are given and received throughout the world, it is the love exchanged through thoughtfulness and sacrifice that is especially dear to us. As is often said, we wish that the spirit of Christmas could last all year. But it is not the gift that is of primary importance. It is the love exchanged.

Love was not invented on the first Christmas, but in a special sense the love that we share at this season did come down at Christmas. While love has always been a human emotion, love, in its deepest meaning, was born at Christmas.

As a carol states, "Love came down at Christmas, love all lovely, love divine; love was born at Christmas: star and angels gave the sign."

The first Christmas was special because in the birth of Jesus divine love was focused for us in a fashion never more clearly perceived. Love came down to be "cradled in straw" so that even the quivering child might have a companion of promise. Love in its emotion would be seen in Jesus' care for his disciples and his mother. Love in its inclusiveness would be demonstrated when a woman taken in adultery was forgiven and when a penitent thief was offered the gift of heaven. Love in its sacrificial nature would never more clearly be seen than in a crucifixion on Calvary. No treasure, however costly, was too great a gift for the Christ Child to give – not even his life. It was in the full offering of himself that he wished to fulfill God's message to us.

And what was that message?

It was the message that love is what life is meant to be about. "God is Love," and it is in the living out of that love in our everyday lives that we find joy, purpose, and hope for this life and the life to come. (1 John 4:8)

Christmas, therefore, is a time for thanksgiving. It is a time to give thanks for love. It is a time to give thanks for the love we share with each other and for the gift of God in Christ. It is a time to give thanks for love which allows us to be forgiven and restored when relationships fail. We celebrate good times, when love is felt; and we celebrate the good news that love can continue after love is lost.

If love is the gift you wish to give at Christmas, rejoice that you have that gift to give. If love is the gift you wish to receive, open your heart to new possibilities. Place yourself at the cradle of the Christ Child and think of all that his gift of love is meant to be. Think of his gentleness. Think of his courage. Think of the generosity of his love. Think of the hope that he gives to all who will receive it.

Can't Find God?

The search to find God is a part of many lives. Some find a relationship with God through their worshiping communities and are grateful that they can speak of God in a personal way. But others are still on their search. They have imagined God as sometimes portrayed in Sunday school lessons as an old man sitting on a throne in heaven ordering the course of the universe. But astronauts didn't find a place called heaven or an old man on a throne. That imagery doesn't work. Some may have thought that God was like a policeman always waiting to catch us when we do something wrong. But why would we choose to worship a God who only makes us feel guilty? Maybe God just created the world and then left everything up to us for good or ill. Many think this is indeed what God did.

Sometimes the reason we don't find God is that we are looking in the wrong place. We tend to think that God is somewhere out there – wherever out there might be. God, if God exists, is viewed as transcendent rather than immanent. So we give up and don't look for God within our own house.

The Mulla Nasrudin in Turkish, Russian, and Middle Ages folklore has many curious teachings that at first may seem stupid but may carry some mystical secret. One quip in this regard is when someone saw Nasrudin searching for something on the ground. "What have you lost, Mulla?" he asked.

"My key," said the Mulla. So they both went down on their knees and looked for it. After a time the other man asked: "Where exactly did you drop it?"

"In my own house."

"Then why are you looking here?"

"There is more light here than inside my own house."

There are probably multiple meanings and applications for this vignette, but it is obvious that the men were looking for the key in the wrong place. Sometimes that's our problem too. We fail to look for God in our own house, our own person. God dwells within each of us; and the more we strive to know our true selves the more acquainted we will become with God. God is the true Self that lives within us.

Spiritual Intentions

Those of us who intentionally pursue the spiritual life can't help but take time for a check-in. How am I doing? Am I a little closer to figuring out this Mystery? Have I turned my life over to the Spirit in some significant way so that the light of Christ shines through me to others? How am I doing, Lord? Do you love me? Do I get any special credit for my good intentions?

This kind of introspection is common especially at the beginning of a year when many are making or already breaking New Year's resolutions. We review our activities in order to take control of our lives to make them positive. Sometimes our new programs for happiness work. Discipline and hard work can produce desired results.

In the spiritual life, however, the process is more than an application of our best efforts. We cannot reach heaven by building a ladder. In fact, we often get in our own way by concentrating on how we are doing rather than presenting ourselves to God in a humble fashion. God is interested in a loving relationship with us rather than handing out merit badges for our good efforts. In our goal for personal achievement we may create absolute answers to spiritual questions so that we can feel secure and certain that everything will work out as desired. But certitude is the opposite of faith. It replaces trust with seeming facts that aren't necessarily so. This is the problem with taking every word of the Bible as literally true, forgetting that the Bible was written by fallible human beings reflecting on their idea of God, right or wrong.

The spiritual journey is not primarily about us but is a willingness to let go of our personal identity to participate in a transpersonal consciousness that we call Spirit. It is an openness to glimpse the Source of All Being – to begin the process of merging into Divine Love. In this process the ego-bound self dies to self to be free to enter into unity consciousness. The process is not one of finding answers but one of discovering humility as we journey the pathway to God.

There is value reflecting on our lives and pursuing good intentions especially if we are on a destructive course. But we need to remember that the identity project is ultimately doomed since it tends to create a false self that is more interested in itself than in the Source that made all things possible. The spiritual process is one of letting go of the self to become one with the Ground of our Being. How this occurs is a mystery, but our surrender allows this grace filled transformation to occur. It is the "ego's journey home to the source of its own Being." (K. D. Singh)

God Cries with Us

When bad things happen to good people one might ask, "Where was God? How could God allow such a thing to happen?" The slaughter of twenty innocent children and six adult staff members at the Sandy Hook Elementary School in Newtown, Connecticut, is a case in point. How can anyone begin to bear the pain born by parents, families, colleagues and friends, and the nation as a whole?

The news media has given us full coverage of this tragic event in December 2012. And now people are trying to answer their own question: "Where was God?" Various answers are given even from the religious community. Some believe that God is always in charge of the world so that if bad things happen it is God's will even if we don't understand the reason. Others say that God, like a good parent, has given us free will to make decisions on our own – some resulting in good works and others bad. We are not God's puppets. The strings have been cut. That's the risk God took. Taking the risk, however, was the only way that we could truly learn to love. Being forced to love is not love. Love requires free choice to be true. It must come freely from the human heart and mind.

Blaming God for the slaughter of innocent people in Newtown turns God into a monster not worthy of worship. We can be grateful that kind of God is not taught to our children in public schools. It provides good reason why we uphold the separation of church and state in government and in our schools. Religion that equates God with Evil is a travesty.

The God of love is more likely to be crying with us when bad things happen on our earthly pilgrimage. Just as we have shed tears for our losses and those of others, so does God feel our pain and cries with us while extending loving arms. Love, God's name, takes no pleasure in the tragic choices that we make whether intentionally or as a result of mental illness. God is certainly not the guilty party in these situations.

There is much in this life for which there are no satisfying answers, but a god who inflicts evil on his children as an act of retribution for who knows what, is not the God of the Christian gospel of good news.

Bitter or Thankful

It is sad when people in the twilight years of their lives turn bitter. Disappointment may be the result of dreams not realized with slight hope of achieving those goals. Others may become bitter because life today is not like the "good old days." They remember when there seemed to be less political turmoil, when people filled the churches, when public violence was scarce and freedom more idyllic. Their previous positive energies have now turned bitter and they see little for which to be thankful.

As we know, change is inevitable. Getting used to new ways can be upsetting to those who are comfortable with the way things were. Some comment, "They don't make cars like they used to." That statement is true no matter which way you look at it. They don't make '57 Chevies and '59 Cadillacs as they used to, and they don't make cars that are likely to need their engines rebuilt at ninety thousand miles. Some people are glad they don't make cars like they used to.

The nostalgia one might have for the past is fine in memory, but turning bitter about the present because things have changed is a choice. Those who live their lives with a spirit of thanksgiving can continue to give thanks for the good things of life, the relationships that remain dear, and focus on the changes that have benefited society in recent years. We may have thought there was more freedom in the United States 50 years ago, but that wasn't true for African Americans, women, and gays and lesbians. We may wish that young people were flocking to our churches as in the past, but we can be grateful that the weariness of many traditional denominations has motivated young people to seek new ways to be "spiritual but not religious," as they say. Just as old fashioned country clubs are losing their appeal and closing, so are traditional churches losing their social and religious appeal. As a leaf must fall and a new bud appear in the spring, so it is with the spiritual cycle of birth, life, death, and re-birth. We may grieve the winter of our lives when all is bare and cold, but spring will come for the young who can rejoice in the life they have been given to enjoy.

The past, present, and future all have their problems and blessings in the rhythm of life. The changing seasons of our lives may bring disappointments, but the good news of Jesus is that we are forgiven and loved by God at any age. The message is not, "Ain't it awful." There is no good news in tireless complaining. Jesus did not come to reiterate how bad we are in order to scare us into salvation through fear, but rather to lure us with love to new life and hope. That is certainly something for which to be thankful, not bitter.

Great Works and Small

On occasion we are motivated to perform some good work that will benefit the welfare of others. Civic leaders do this on a regular basis. Churches and social agencies continue to aid the poor and needy. Health workers strive to keep us healthy. Some of this altruistic work is acknowledged by the community, and other good deeds are accomplished quietly.

And then there are the mundane activities of our daily lives that seem to take up most of our time. There are meals to prepare, children to raise, shopping, the routine of our work, etc. Because most of our time may seem ordinary we don't have the satisfaction of performing any great works – just small works.

If you sometimes feel this way, think of Brother Lawrence (1611-1691), a Carmelite lay brother who spent forty years of his life in a monastery kitchen in Paris. There was nothing particularly special about him. He came from a humble background and had little or no formal education. He would not be remembered in history had it not been for M. de Beaufort, a visiting official on the staff of the cardinal of Paris, who happened to initiate conversation with Brother Lawrence and was astonished by the depth of his spiritual wisdom. "According to Brother Lawrence, wherever we might find ourselves, whatever the task at hand, we should perform our duties with a consciousness of God's loving presence. With such awareness all our activities are hallowed; we would thus find ourselves in a state of continuous prayer or conversation with God."

While we might wonder whether or not we are performing any great works, Brother Lawrence made no distinction between great works and small. As he liked to observe, "God regards not the greatness of the work, but the love with which it is performed."

In all we do, great or small, may we do it with love.

Good Friday

Elie Weisel who survived the holocaust wrote a horrifying memoir of his life as a German Jew under the terror of Nazism. One day in his life in the prison camp stands out for him for the cruelty and darkness. As difficult as the story of that day is to read and endure, I share it with you.

"The three victims mounted together onto the scaffold. The three necks were placed at the same moment within the nooses. 'Long live liberty!' cried the two adults. But the young boy was silent. 'Where is God? Where is he?' someone behind me asked. At a sign from the head of the camp, the three chairs tipped over. Total silence followed throughout the camp. On the horizon, the sun was setting...Then the march past began. The two adults were no longer alive. Their tongues hung swollen, blue tinged. But the third rope was still moving; being so light, the child was still alive...For more than half an hour he stayed there struggling between life and death, dying in slow agony under our eyes. And we had to look him full in the face. He was still alive when I passed in front of him. His tongue was still red; his eyes were not yet glazed. Behind me I heard the same man asking: 'Where is God now?' And I heard a voice within me answer him: 'Where is He? Here He is – He is hanging here on this gallows...'"

Where is God in the face of pain, cruelty, injustice, all the nightmare horrors, great and small of this life? Where is he?

God hears our questions. And God replies. That reply is the cross of Jesus.

Scott Lee, a priest friend of mine, noted that on a hillside in Palestine an innocent man was tortured to death. "Does it take away the pain of other deaths?" he asked. No, it does not. "Does it make our loss of those we love less painful?" It does not. "Does it explain to us why there should be pain and loss in the world?" It does not.

"What the cross of Jesus does do is stand as a towering witness to us that God participates in our pain; that there is no darkness so dark that God does not wait for us there. There is no evil the human heart can devise so evil that God will not match it with God's love; that there is no terror so great that God has not already known it and consecrated it.

Many questions remain unanswered. But for now, while we do not have answers, we have the mystery of God's response. It is the cross."

If you hear a voice within you asking, "Where is God now?" listen to your heart, a voice of hope within saying, "Here I am, hanging on this gallows where human fear and cruelty and greed and hatred have put me. I am hanging here on this gallows in spite of all your fear and hatred with my arms still outstretched to you in love...and no terror can ever change that."

And so we call this Friday "Good."

'Outdo one another in showing honor'

The scriptures are filled with exhortations to love one another. An example from St. Paul is found in his Epistle to the Romans: "Let love be genuine; hate what is evil, hold fast to what is good; love one another with mutual affection; outdo one another in showing honor." (Romans 12:9-10)

Some like to think of this as an incentive to outdo one another with love. Love is meant to be abundant. It is in love shared that we experience the face of God in one another.

An ancient rabbinic story tells of this love in action. My friend, Matthew Corkern, retells the parable like this:

"Long, long ago, when the world was still young, two brothers shared a field and a mill. Each night they divided equally the grain they had ground together during the day. One brother lived alone; the other had a wife and many children. Now the single brother thought to himself, 'It really is not fair that we divide the grain evenly, as I have only myself to care for, and my brother has many mouths to feed.' So each night he secretly took some of his grain to his brother's granary.

But the married brother said to himself, 'It really is not fair that we divide the grain evenly, as I have children to care for me in my old age, but my brother will have no one.' So every night he secretly took some of his grain to his brother's granary. As you may have guessed, both of the brothers found their supply of grain mysteriously replenished each morning.

Then one night they met each other halfway between the two houses and suddenly realized what had been happening all those years. They embraced with great affection as the truth dawned upon them. Legend has it that God witnessed their meeting and proclaimed: 'This is a holy place, a place of love, and here it is that my temple shall be built.' And so it was that the first temple was constructed on that site still revered to this day as the most sacred location for the Holy of Holies in Jerusalem."

What a joy it is when we discover holy places founded on love. As John writes, "Beloved, let us love one another, because love is from God; everyone who loves is born of God and knows God. Whoever does not love does not know God, for God is love." (1 John 4: 7-8)

Alleluia. Christ is Risen

"Alleluia. Christ is risen. The Lord is risen indeed. Alleluia." This is the greeting many share on Easter Day. It will continue to welcome worshipers during the Easter season. It is an exclamation that the Spirit of Christ is alive and well. Christians don't gather on Sundays just to remember an event two thousand years ago. We worship to give thanks that God's loving presence continues to be with us individually and in community, and that as God was in Christ, so is Christ's presence within each one of us.

On that first Easter morning, Mary Magdalene came to the tomb of Jesus and saw that the stone covering the tomb had been removed. She ran and found Peter and John to come and see, fearing that Jesus' body had been stolen. They found the linen wrappings, but did not understand at the time that Jesus would rise from the dead. The disciples returned to their homes but Mary stood weeping. As she wept, two angels appeared with whom she spoke; and then as she turned around, she saw a man appearing to be the gardener. Wondering if he had been the one who took away Jesus' body, she was startled when he said to her, "Mary." It was then that she knew it was Jesus, risen from the dead. (John 20:1-18)

Some people have assumed that Jesus' risen body was a resuscitated corpse. If it had been, Mary would have recognized him right away. In other resurrection accounts Jesus is not immediately known. On the road to Emmaus, for example, on that same day, two disciples were walking along talking about what had taken place with Jesus. Jesus himself came near and went with them. The disciples didn't recognize him at first but became suspicious about his identity when he began interpreting things about himself in the Scriptures. They urged him to stay with them since the day was almost over. He stayed, and when they were at the table together, "He took bread, blessed, and broke it, and gave it to them. Then their eyes were opened, and they recognized him; and he vanished from their sight." (Luke 24:13-35) His followers in these encounters discovered his identity as he called one by name and shared a meal with the other two in the breaking of bread. His presence was recognized, not by the nature of his appearance, but in the essence of his spiritual power.

I find this comforting. First, when we rise to new life after our deaths, our physical bodies won't be of any use to us. It is the spiritual body that moves closer to the very heart of God. And it is in our life together, in the breaking of the bread and in fellowship with one another, that we recognize the Christ spirit in our daily lives. It isn't often that we hear of visual appearances of Jesus in modern days, but reputable people have experienced such phenomena. No doubt these appearances are much like those that the early disciples and St. Paul experienced.

One of the blessings that Christians enjoy is experiencing Christ's presence when gathered for worship or fellowship, in service and outreach programs, and in working together to provide resources to support the mission and ministry of Christ. It may scare us a little, but God's identity was born into us, and the recognition of that essence is often discovered by others seeing it in us and helping us to nurture its growth. God's love and new life are with us to be discovered in our prayers, in our life together, and in our service to others.

Following the example of Mary Magdalene, the first evangelist, we have the opportunity to run after anyone who might welcome the good news of Jesus. As the opening words of a book by a scholar friend of mine state, "You are forgiven. Nothing more. Nothing less." (L. Wm. Countryman) Everything that can mess up our lives was absorbed by Jesus on his cross and was buried with him. His Spirit was renewed to let us know that God has the last word. And that word is one of hope and new life. The resurrection is witness to the fact that we get a second, a third, a fourth and many more chances to be a part of God's life, especially as we discover that presence in the person of Jesus.

The resurrection was not a one-time event. It is witness to the reality that the Good Fridays of our lives and even death itself cannot end our journey with God. God, as revealed in Jesus, is alive and well, carrying us forward to comfort and sustain us, and at the last, to bring us to eternal life.

Biblical Authority or Biblical Tyranny?

A brilliant New Testament scholar, L. William Countryman, wrote a book titled *Biblical Authority or Biblical Tyranny?* He asks what the authority of the Bible is for Christians. What do we mean when we say that the Bible is inspired? Infallible? The word of God? What is the relationship between the Bible and the Church? Who decides how to interpret the Scriptures?

These are some of the questions he deals with which are asked frequently by those interested in religion and for which there are multiple answers. He notes that there are Christians who claim that their Christianity, and theirs alone, is truly biblical. "These Christians imagine that the nature of biblical authority is perfectly clear; they often speak of Scripture as inerrant. In fact, however, they have tacitly abandoned the authority of Scripture in favor of a conservative Protestant theology shaped largely in the nineteenth century. This fundamentalist theology they buttress with strings of quotations to give it a biblical flavor, but it predetermines their reading of Scripture so completely that one cannot speak of the Bible as having any independent voice in their churches."

"The majority of American Christians, on the other hand, belong to churches which do not make such exclusive claims either for themselves or for their interpretations of Scripture. These churches, for the most part, came to terms with historical-critical study of the Bible quite some time ago; and they have recognized that no one theological system can adequately represent the Scriptures and that the Scriptures, in turn, cannot totally determine theology. This does not mean that these churches have neglected Scripture, but it does mean that they have no simple explanation of the place of the Bible in modern Christianity."

"There is a half-conscious Biblicism in much of American Christianity which wants to treat Scripture as if it were infallible and, therefore, identical with God. This position is basically contrary to what the Bible reveals about itself. There is a natural and understandable human desire to have some authority available to us that would answer all questions. What God has given us, instead, is a word that prompts more questions than it answers. In Scripture, God has uttered for us not the last word but the first – a word designed to set us off on pilgrimage, in pursuit of that life that God has willed for us to have."

Professor Countryman argues that the Bible's authority becomes tyrannical when we try to use it in ways it was never meant to be used, for the real authority of the Bible lies in its power to bring about our conversion, and "the Bible makes sense to us fully only as we come to be fully transformed by it."

The books included in the Bible were selected from many available at councils of the church in the Fourth Century. Paul's letters, for example, were not written to become scripture but as a way to communicate with the infant churches being established. They are nevertheless helpful to us to understand Paul's mind and the ministry of the early church. The Bible as a whole was written by people expressing their understanding of the nature of God. This understanding is a changing revelation that continues with us in our day as we reflect on biblical insights as they might apply to our own lives.

When we read the Bible it is important to remember that "God did not give us a summary of belief, a convenient statement of fundamentals, a list of propositions to be believed or of rules to be obeyed. God has given us instead, the wonderfully deep, convoluted, and perplexing Bible – as rich in mystery as it is in light."

Let Me Live until I Die

Many people contend with serious illness. Perhaps this is true for you, a friend, or relative. Assuming proper medical attention is being provided, you may wish to add your prayers for the one suffering. A cure would certainly be the first hope. But if the illness appears to be terminal you may wonder what to pray for – a miracle or a painless death. A prayer for God's healing presence and comfort is certainly in order.

A noted African-American Franciscan sister, Thea Bowman, faced this issue in her own life. After having a splendid career as a spellbinding speaker, storyteller, preacher and performer, she was diagnosed in 1984 as suffering from breast cancer. She continued her ministry as best she could, and her audiences detected an even more personal and poignant confession of faith as she approached what was for her a terminal illness. Dealing with her own question on how to pray she said, "When I first found out I had cancer, I didn't know what to pray for. I didn't know if I should pray for healing or life or death. Then I found peace in praying for what my folks call 'God's perfect will.' As it evolved, my prayer has become, 'Lord, let me live until I die.' By that I mean I want to live, love, and serve fully until death comes. If that prayer is answered…how long really doesn't matter. Whether it's just a few months or a few years is really immaterial."

Asked how she made sense out of her suffering, she answered, "I don't make sense of suffering. I try to make sense of life…I try each day to see God's will…I console myself with the old Negro spiritual: 'Sooner will be done the troubles of this world. I'm going home to live with God.'"

Sister Thea died in 1990 at the age of fifty-three having lived an inspirational life for others. Her prayer, 'Lord, let me live until I die,' is a good prayer for each of us whether or not we contend with an illness. Each day lived fully for as many days as we are given can bring joy through love and service to others and satisfy our desire to live a life worth living. (See *All Saints*, Robert Ellsberg)

Hospitality

Hospitality is a big part of Christian living. By welcoming others we express the love and generosity that Jesus taught. It is a reminder to us that when we welcome anyone we are welcoming Christ at the same time. In Jesus' words, "I swear to God, if they welcome the person I send, they welcome me; and if they welcome me, they welcome the one who sent me." (Matt. 10:40)

Matthew's version of this hospitality speaks of reception and rewards commensurate with the people they welcome. Jesus' remark promises a reward for even the most modest gesture of hospitality toward his disciples: "Whoever gives even a cup of cold water to one of these little ones in the name of a disciple – truly I tell you, none of these will lose their reward." (Matt. 10:42)

When I think of Jesus' statement, "Whoever welcomes you welcomes me, and whoever welcomes me welcomes the one who sent me," I think of Mother Teresa whose life was devoted to caring for the poor and needy, and who looked for Christ within each person – even in their distressing disguise.

She tells the story about one of her sisters in the Order who had just graduated from the university. She came from a well-to-do family that lived outside of India.

According to the rule of the Order, the very next day after joining the society, the postulants must go to the home for the dying destitute in Calcutta. Before this postulant went, Mother Teresa told her, "You saw the priest during the Mass – with what love, with what delicate care he touched the body of Christ. Make sure you do the same thing when you get to the home, because Jesus is there in a distressing disguise."

So the new sister went, and after three hours, she came back. That girl from the university, who had seen and understood so many things, came to Mother Teresa's room with such a beautiful smile on her face. She said, "For three hours I've been touching the body of Christ!"

And Mother Teresa said, "What did you do? What happened?"

She said, "They brought a man from the street who had fallen into a drain and had been there for some time. He was covered with maggots and dirt and wounds. And though I found it very difficult, I cleaned him, and I knew I was touching the body of Christ!" She knew! (*In the Heart of the World*, Mother Teresa)

Our welcoming, looking for the face of Christ within each other and those we are yet to meet, may not be as poignant as Teresa's story, but it is the same hospitality that Jesus asks us to offer as we greet one another in the name of Christ. It doesn't require any conspicuous labels of generosity. It simply requires a generous heart that sees even the stranger as a brother or sister.

Silent to Be Heard

Sometimes oxymoronic advice can be very true. A case in point is the writer Stanislaw Lec's comment: "Sometimes you have to be silent to be heard." I don't know what the original intent of this comment was, but there are occasions in social life when remaining silent speaks louder than if we had spoken. For those who speak it might take some guessing to determine the reason for someone else's silence. The reason could be as simple as having laryngitis and to speak would hurt one's throat. The silence could be an indication that someone feels left out of the conversation and regrets that no one has invited him/her to join in. It could also mean that to join in the conversation could mar your own sense of integrity. If the conversation has turned into hurtful gossip you might want to refrain from adding to the tar and feathering. Remaining silent might make you feel uncomfortable, and later to be accused of being a "goodie, goodie." But your silence may speak louder than if you rose in defense of the person being belittled. You've made your point by remaining silent.

In the Epistle of James we read that the tongue "is a small member, yet it boasts of great exploits. How great a forest is set ablaze by a small fire! And the tongue is a fire." (James 3:5-6) The author is warning us to be careful about the things we say. Certainly our speech has been used to teach and to inspire others. But on occasion the tongue can get us into trouble. Remaining silent may be the best choice. Our silence will be heard, but not in a detrimental way.

In our private lives there are also times when we should shut down noisy conversations with ourselves – what we are going to say to others, how we are feeling, worry about all the things we have to do, etc. It may be that we have to be silent to give the Spirit a chance to speak in the depths of our hearts. Silent time isn't wasted time. It is a time to listen. Conversations where no one listens are a waste of time. Nothing is communicated. Relationships are not enhanced. And when we seem to be doing all the talking to ourselves, enter a private room, be quiet, let go of all that is bothering you, and free up the rumble of your thoughts. Just be silent in the presence of God. God's first language is silence, so let God have a chance to speak to you uninterrupted. Sometimes we have to be silent to hear.

Taken by Surprise

Leon Trotsky, best known for his political activities, was also a good thinker and writer. He observed, "Old age is the most unexpected of all the things that can happen to a man." Indeed, when we are young old age seems so far away that we seldom think about it. Then, having found life much too time-consuming, we unexpectedly look in the mirror and discover that old age has appeared. We may feel like we are forty-two, but how did we get to seventy-two in so few years?

This experience occurs for most who live to become elders. The sudden arrival at a new age makes one ask questions about one's life. Where have I been? What about my dreams? What's next?

Old age is a time to reflect on our lives. It may also be a time to cope with new challenges, such as adjustment to limitations and the need to let go. At first we may think of this new age only in terms of personal losses, but turning to positive aspects of this chapter in our lives we discover that the aging process is not just a matter of loss but an opportunity to live at a more leisurely pace, to read and to pursue new questions, and to bring to others the wisdom gained through experience. One doesn't have to limit one's thinking to issues of the past, holding on to memories with nostalgia, but can continue to be immersed in the issues of the present day.

Joan Chittister in her splendid book, *The Gift of Years*, notes that it is the elders in a society that are really "the only ones who are free to tell the truth. They have nothing to lose now: not status, not striving, not money, not power. They are meant to be the prophets of a society, its compass, its truth-tellers."

A burden of these later years in life is to assume that the future is already over. The future may be now, but it's not over until our spirits are released into the hands of God. God is present in the "now" of our lives at any age. Each moment is a time to be alive, to be ourselves, and to be grateful for grace-filled years. It is a time when we can enjoy the luxury of reflective spiritual growth. The best of our values can be strengthened. Even as we melt into God, our last conversations can be times "to be honest, to be loving, to be open, to be grateful, to be patient, to be lovable and loving and loved." Robert Browning's inspirational words regarding the twilight years have been helpful to many as they approached their elder years.

Grow old along with me!
The best is yet to be,
The last of life, for which the first was made;
Our times are in His hand
Who saith 'A whole I planned,
Youth shows but half;
Trust God: see all, nor be afraid!'

The Gift of a Child

The birth of a child is a joyous and solemn occasion in the life of a family. It is also an occasion for rejoicing in the Christian community. In some churches there is a service of thanksgiving for the birth of a child and a dedication of the child to God. Children are often baptized and made members of the Body of Christ while still young. In other churches the baptism is postponed until the child can make a personal profession of faith. In churches where little children are baptized the profession of faith comes in a service called confirmation.

Children join a family through their biological parents or through adoption. For those families who adopt a child this occasion can be an answer to prayer. In the Episcopal Church there is a service wherein the new parents receive the child as their own; and if there are other siblings, they receive the child as a brother or sister. After offering heartfelt thanks for the joyful and solemn responsibility which has been given to this family, the minister, holding or taking the child by the hand, gives the child to the mother or father, saying: "As God has made us his children by adoption and grace, may you receive (name) as your own son (daughter). Then one or both parents say these or similar words: "May God, the Father of all, bless our child (name), and us who have given to him our family name, that we may live together in love and affection; through Jesus Christ our Lord." Amen.

Adoption has been a blessing in my extended family in which four of our family members have been adopted. We are now connected in a rainbow of color with English, African American, and American Indian combinations.

Adoption is a blessing for so many children who might otherwise not have the nurture of a loving home. Single people and same sex couples are also bringing this joy to children through adoption. As we are all adopted as God's children, it is a privilege that we can adopt one another as our own. Jesus taught us that whoever receives a little child in the name of Christ receives Christ himself. When we receive Christ as a little child we have the gift of bringing that child up "to love all that is true and noble, just and pure, lovable and gracious, excellent and admirable, following the example of our Lord and Savior, Jesus Christ."

Jesus Wasn't a Christian

It is easy to assume that Jesus of Nazareth was a Christian. After all, a religion was named in his honor. This name for the followers of Jesus did not occur, however, until years after Jesus' death. Jesus himself was a Jew hoping to bring new dimensions of love to Judaism. His disciples declared that the future of Judaism was not in adherence to the leadership of the scribes and Pharisees but with Jesus. They understood Jesus to be the Christ, the anointed one of God. These disciples were a sect of Judaism and eventually became a separate group known as Christians. The term "Christian" was never used by Jesus. The word first appears in the Book of Acts: "The disciples were first called Christians in Antioch." (Acts 11:26)

Another assumption many Christians have is that one must be baptized as a Christian in order to escape the fires of hell. If this were the case then all of the Old Testament leaders including Abraham, Moses, David, and the prophets are now burning because they were not Christians. They were Jews just like Jesus.

Assumptions can get us into trouble. If we think God adheres to the exclusive limitations we place on God's love, we end up with a theology not worth living. The cosmic presence of God known through faith, prayer, and contemplation is witness to the Spirit's presence in everything, everywhere and at every moment. As the French Benedictine monk Henri le Saux (Swami Abhishiktananda) has written, "To live by faith is to have the mind open and awakened to the mystery of God – of God in himself certainly and first of all, but no less to the mystery of his manifestation in the universe."

This pervasive experience of God is known by people in every age who carry various religious labels, and by those who claim no religious affiliation. One does not have to have a Christian passport to feel the presence of the Spirit in creation, in one another, and in both transcendent and intimate ways. God cannot be confined to the limitations we place on God in order to enhance our need to feel special at the expense of billions of God's beloved children throughout the world.

God's presence with us in human form is not limited to the presence seen in Jesus. God wants to know what it is like to be human within each one of us regardless of the labels we attach to ourselves. In each case God would like to see through our eyes and have us see through God's eyes toward one another in love. Such love spends little time condemning others. It looks to see the Spirit of God within everyone. Certainly there is no need to condemn the God who dwells within us all.

Matter Matters

Archbishop William Temple, a former archbishop of Canterbury, said: "Christianity is the most materialistic of all religions." He was reflecting on the fact that Christianity emphasizes God's presence in creation and within each of us. Jesus' life was the finest example of God being incarnate in human form and in the everyday matters of our lives. God did not set the world in motion and then forget us. God is present in creation, in matter, and sees it to be good. Matter thus matters.

There is a tendency in some religious expressions to minimize the material world and to concentrate primarily on the spiritual world. This dualism can be found in most religions, even in Christianity. Some will point to a few passages from St. Paul's letters that seem to uphold this point of view. But many of us see Paul's emphasis as only a way to uphold our spiritual lives which are often neglected when we become too encumbered with the material aspects of our lives. The goal, however, is to respect both our human and spiritual natures. The Creator determined to put matter and spirit together. Both are good and sacred. God has overcome the human-divine gap in the Christ Mystery.

Richard Rohr has written, "This is Christianity's only completely unique message. Full incarnation is what distinguishes us from all other religions. This is our only real trump card, and for the most part, we have not yet played it. History, the planet – and other religions – have only suffered as a result. Incarnationalism does not put you in competition with any other religions but, in fact, allows you to see God in all things, including them! It mandates that you love and respect all others."

The challenge for us is to embrace creation, to see God in all things and all people, and to bring the dark areas of our lives into the light of Christ.

No Exceptions to God's Love

The Judeo-Christian tradition has taught that human beings are made in the image and likeness of God. "So God created humankind in his image, in the image of God he created them; male and female he created them." (Genesis 1:27) By this we understand that a little bit of God dwells within each of us. In creation God certainly had a great imagination by creating us in a variety of colors, bringing us up in many different cultures, and giving us as many personalities as there are individuals. Apparently God wanted to know what it is like to experience human life through our eyes so that we might experience God through God's eyes.

One can attempt to figure out one image for God, perhaps as a father. But God has chosen to become incarnate in our images to make God's gift of love personal for each human being. God is not an object but is in every person and within the creation itself.

If we take this incarnation seriously, then the Divine Presence appears in multiple images. God is male and female, straight and gay, black, white, red, tan, yellow, etc. The children of God are Christians, Jews, Hindus, Muslims, Buddhists, and pagans. Certainly no other God created people who differ from us. We all carry God's DNA. There are no exceptions to this spark of God planted within each person.

It is true that we don't always express the benevolence of God in our daily living, and we certainly are not God's puppets. We have the ability to make choices and to express ourselves. But deep within us is the presence of God seeking to continue the creative process by bringing us more nearly into the image and likeness of God which is Love.

It seems futile to spend time trying to decide who and who isn't going to heaven or hell. The fact is that God dwells within each of us whether or not we display God's goodness. It is unimaginable that God would condemn God's own self. The God within us will live forever. God's love has no exceptions since that Love abides within each person.

Freedom

It seems evident that no nation values freedom as much as America. We celebrate Independence Day with gusto recalling the Declaration of Independence. Fireworks and festivities make this holiday a grand occasion.

Freedom is a cherished national gift allowing citizens to go about their business with the right to make choices and to determine a beneficial course of action for their lives. We believe "that all men are created equal, that they are endowed by their Creator with certain unalienable Rights, that among these are Life, Liberty, and the pursuit of Happiness."

Freedom is also a personal responsibility. It causes us to ask questions about our lives. What demands my attention? Am I killing myself at work while searching for happiness? Am I a slave to some addiction? Have my political or religious ideals become so narrow that I don't have the freedom to learn something new?

St. Paul wrote about freedom but realistically knew that we simply have the freedom to choose our slavery. Will it be a commitment to work for positive goals or will we submit to actions that tear us apart and harm others? He notes that we

are slaves to the one we obey, for good or ill.
(Romans 6:16-18)

Some people fear freedom because of its demands. How would you feel if you were "content to live without goals, satisfied that living is enough?" (J. Kavanaugh) Do you scoff at titles, laugh at greed, forget about needing a monument at your grave? Are those freedoms you embrace?

We might also ask if our joys have become our slavery. Is the golf game worth the sacrifice of family relationships? Is the desire to make money our real joy, not what money can do to help others? Am I a slave to selfishness under the guise of being free? Am I morally free to hold on to my prejudices that minimize the value of others? Does my freedom have the right to infringe on the freedom of others?

Edward Hays, who often has curious tales to tell from history, noted in his *Book of Wonders* that the Statue of Liberty was originally designed for the 1870 celebration of the opening of the Suez Canal. The statue was of an Egyptian peasant woman of the Nile wearing a Muslim face veil. She held her torch high, symbolic of Egypt bringing light to Asia. When the wealthy Arab prince benefactor financing the statue went bankrupt, Frederic Bartholdi (sculptor) was forced to inventively redesign his statue. Removing her veil, he made her into the Statue of Liberty, whose torch was now to enlighten the world. Hays asks what the effects would be if tomorrow a Muslim-veiled Miss Liberty would appear on patriotic floats in countless parades, and in displays for Fourth of July sales.

We might ask ourselves what veils we need to remove to honor the dignity and freedom of those who differ from ourselves. In government, is it valid to use one's political party's power to redraw voting districts to limit the effect of the opposition's vote? If you can afford health insurance, is it right to preserve your financial freedom by failing to contribute to the health needs of the poor? If you think you are right from a religious point of view, is it a valid exercise of your freedom to condemn those who would choose mercy?

Freedom from some form of slavery is hard to maintain. Perhaps the key to unlocking our chains is to know that we walk a fine line between freedom and slavery. Russell Hoban says in *Turtle Diary*, "Prisons are all we know how to make." Maybe we can discover an alternative that relies on the winds of the Spirit to set us free.

Religious Child Abuse

We are horrified to hear of children being abused. The culprits can be parents and relatives, neighbors, even community leaders and clergy. While the abuse suffered is often physical, mental and psychological, abuse can leave lasting scars as well.

In my pastoral ministry I have worked with adults who were abused as children by being brainwashed into believing violent images of the nature of God. They have heard that by their very birth they are depraved. Even a newborn infant is destined for hell if not baptized. They learned that God watches every move they make and is ready to condemn them for every fault. God for them became the ultimate policeman, and not the friendly kind we so often meet. As children they didn't experience healthy self-esteem. And ironically, they were supposed to love this tyrannical God.

In adulthood, some who were abused with negative images of God realize that such a mean-spirited god has nothing to do with the God of love Jesus taught. Meanwhile, they have difficulty erasing these old tapes taught to them in childhood. Learning that they are beloved children of God is interrupted with negative images from childhood that tear down their self-esteem. Some dealing with this spiritual conflict yearn to love themselves so they can love and respect others. You can't truly love others until you have compassion for yourself.

Mental and spiritual child abuse by the religious community is regrettable. It can damage the health of adults when these negative tapes play again in their consciousness at unexpected moments. And learning to let go of these painful images of God takes prayer and practice. When negative thoughts arise, one needs to identify them – but not fight with them, and then let them go as gently as possible. It is only by holding on to them that continuing damage can be done. Forgiveness for those who abused one's spirit may take longer, but the desire to forgive can be turned over to God to accomplish. If your prayer to forgive only reminds you of the pain, let God do the praying for you to grant blessing rather than cursing. This approach takes time but can begin to free one to move forward in positive ways.

Life is a beautiful gift from God to be enjoyed. Our own violence shouldn't be projected on to God and taught to our children. God's primary identity is Love, and the test of that love is abundant forgiveness.

Innocence

On occasion you may wish that you could go back to a time in your life when you felt the wonder of innocence. The world was beautiful, you were loved, and deep within, you heard a still small voice saying you were okay. You may remember moments when you seemed to be surrounded by grace, although you might not have known the meaning of that word. When you said your prayers as a child you couldn't see God, but this undisclosed Being was present for you as you prayed for mommy and daddy, siblings and friends – and your pets too. You didn't question this reality in your little life, and you didn't try to explain it. It just was. And in your daily life you discovered new things – a yellow rose blooming under a bright blue sky, a cricket, a robin, and a stink bug.

I remember moments like this when my awareness of spiritual realities just happened – as the sun filled my bedroom with light, in viewing leaves in rainbow colors lining the banks of the Hudson River, and singing chants with monks at Holy Cross monastery. I didn't create these occasions. They were gifts from God; and in my unencumbered innocence I felt the wonder and mystery of God that remains tethered to my soul even through successive years of ups and downs.

Returning to a time of innocence is about as productive as "revirgination." It just doesn't happen – except in our memories. The purity of those days has been marred with the lingering weight of past mistakes, absolved or yet to be forgiven. Hopefully you have heard Jesus' words on the lips of those offended: "You are forgiven." And if your life is still in recovery to be rid of demons – perhaps not the usual demons of addictive behaviors, but maybe the demons of guilt, worthlessness, or hopelessness. Where are the days, you might ask, when I didn't have to struggle with my life and with others, and just knew that I was standing on holy ground, the Ground of my Being – God.

Christian Wiman in his beautiful book *My Bright Abyss* writes of his struggle to retain that space in his heart that once heard a still, small voice saying not his name so much as his nature, in a wordless but lucid un-triumphant absolute of "yes." Hearing that affirmation in his soul has sustained him in the dark and illuminated issues of his anticipated death from cancer. Somehow this "something" remains within us, "voiceless even as we voice our deepest faith, doubt, fear, and dreams."

Revisiting this place of innocence in our memory can be a healing experience. We can't go home, so to speak, because the past has given way to present time, and things have changed. But we can remember when God was real without explanation: when our thoughts were white and open. And in recalling that space, healing may penetrate to the present moment. Our deepest faith, doubt, fear, and dreams can be felt in the now of our lives, and the pure reality known in our innocence can wipe the slate clean. We don't have to live in the jungle of our thoughts. We can relax into the mystery of the unknown, the Cloud of Unknowing, yet known mysteriously in the depths of our hearts.

Indulge yourselves in the memories of your innocence, and let those times speak to you again. As a book title suggests, *All I Really Need to Know I Learned in Kindergarten*. (R. Fulghum) In the first half of life we learn what we think we're meant to know; and in the second half we learn to unlearn what we learned. We have to revisit the kindergarten years of our lives, when we could trust fully, when God seemed real without explanation, when the "still small voice" spoke clearly – to a little child. The kingdom of God is known in this simplicity, faith, and love.

A Divided Life

When we are young we tend to be less introspective about our lives and think of ourselves as well put together. It's only later in life that we begin to examine who we are – where we have been and how we would like to live in the future. Some who reflect on this issue discover that they are leading a divided life or double life. For the public they present one image of their identity, but secretly that identity does not match the person inside. Wearing a mask for others becomes a burden making them feel lonely inside. They ask, "Would people love me if they knew who I truly am?"

We often hide our true identities from each other being afraid, as Parker Palmer puts it, "that our inner light will be extinguished or our inner darkness exposed." Some live with this fear for years; but when on retreat or a vacation there's a respite when they don't have to be anyone but themselves. Being away gives a chance to listen to that inner "still, small voice" of God speaking in the depths of one's heart. This voice already knows who we are, so there is no need to put on a front. And even when the divided life is discovered, with its light and darkness, the voice says, "I love you," and I want you to be whole. With this assurance one may venture out to imagine what it would be like to be whole – to be only one person. The risk is that our inner darkness would be exposed, and our light challenged, but we wouldn't have to pretend to be someone we're not. We could say good-bye to the unwelcome guest of our identity.

This divided life is felt for some business executives who feel obligated to maintain a strong public image and orienting their activities to getting ahead and being a success for the company and for themselves. The sensitive element of their lives, however, may be turned off. They become tough when they wish they could be gentle. Housewives sometimes feel they are missing out on life when their home life and volunteering prevents them from developing a career that is burning to be expressed. Young adults are challenged to come to terms with their sexual identity, struggling to live out what they are supposed to be even if they discover they are gay.

Learning to be honest to God and to ourselves is a life long project, but it's worth the risk to become whole inside. Our pretending will be found out sooner or later. God only wants the person we are, not the one we pretend to be. To achieve this end we have to have the humility to accept our gifts and talents – the light, and the dark side of our personalities as well. Acceptance of the dark side will keep us humble and honest.

You may wish you were someone else, but as a Yiddish proverb says:

"If I try to be like him, who will be like me?" And as a learned holy rabbi once told his disciples, "When I get to heaven God isn't going to ask me, 'Rabbi Yosef, why weren't you more like Moses?' No, God will ask me, 'Rabbi Yosef, why weren't you more like the Yosef whom I created?'"

May God help each of us to become the person we were created to be.

A Gentle Moment

Christmas is a splendid time for stories and nostalgia. In our celebrations we remember good times past and create rich new memories. In particular, our generous and gentle selves reappear. We exchange gifts and host parties to share friendship and love. It is a time when we also recall the birth of one whose life was generous and gentle, especially toward the poor and weak. We revisit the crèche and remember the coming of a savior in the simplest of manners – in a stable, in the company of shepherds and sheep. The wise men visit, but even the prowess of their kingdoms is humbled before the child of God.

Perhaps you have imagined being present at Jesus' birth. How were you able to assist Mary, Joseph, and the babe?

Pope John XXIII's Christmas meditation, written when he was a young seminarian, speaks to me as we might have been if we had been at the manger.

"Mary and Joseph, knowing the hour is near, are turned away by the townsfolk and go out into the fields to look for a shelter. I am a poor shepherd; I have only a wretched stable, a small manger, some wisps of straw. I offer all these to you, be pleased to come into my poor hovel. I offer you my heart; my soul is poor and bare of virtues, the straws of so many imperfections will prick you and make you weep – but oh, my Lord, what can you expect? This little is all I have. I am touched by your poverty, I am moved to tears, but I have nothing better to offer you. Jesus, honor my soul with your presence, adorn it with your graces. Burn this straw and change it into a soft couch for your most holy body."

Taking ourselves back to the folklore of those days may seem sentimental, but I think that in an often hard world it is good to remember the simple, the soft and sacred. It's too easy to be success driven, competitive to the point of abuse. Perhaps by contrast there is something to be said for those who step back from power to listen and help.

On Christmas morning, how can we open ourselves to receive this Holy Child? What can we give in thanksgiving? If we were shepherds we could provide a stable or bring a lamb. If wise men we could do our part. Perhaps our best response is to give as the carol suggests: "I can give him, give my heart." (Christina Rossetti, "In the bleak mid-winter")

Cat on the Lap

Perhaps you have a cat. You may have stories to tell about your feline friend including moments with the cat on your lap. There is petting and purring and a shared bond of affection. A sudden sound, however, alerts your little friend that it's time for a change. Another occasion will come, however, when the only sounds heard will be of gentle strokes.

I've lived with cats for many years. My father used to like them especially because of their independence. He was a very independent person and shared a mutual spirit with his friend Pennie. My favorite as a child was Ferdie, a big orange cat with an affectionate flair. My earliest grieving occurred when Ferdie got hit by a car. It was hard for me to forgive the old lady in the cul-de-sac who hit him with her 1936 Ford coupe.

Pets are certainly a part of life's more pleasant moments. They have personalities that can vary from sweet cuddly furry friends to guard dogs prepared to snap at anyone provoking harm. Depending on your situation you learn to love or to respect your pet.

There is a proverb that reads: "The righteous one is aware of the soul of his animal, and the evil withhold their compassion." (Proverbs 12:10) It is an example of the compassion we can learn from our pets and the lack of concern missing from those with an evil spirit. Many have learned compassion from the care of a pet. The pet in turn can teach us unconditional love. Loving pets take us as we are. If only we could share that same attitude with people.

Celebrating the gift of pets is another of God's many blessings. I hope you have opportunities to give thanks for your cats, dogs, rabbits, horses, etc. Remember, when it comes to cats, "Those who dislike cats will be carried to the cemetery in the rain." (Dutch Proverb)

Compassion

Compassion is an essential quality of our religious life. It is the means by which we enter into the suffering of others, and by that participation are able to bring healing and comfort. Developing a compassionate heart is what we are meant to be about, for as we risk forgetting ourselves and our own safety we enter into the heart of God through those we serve. Compassion is an expression of the stupendous love of God which we are privileged to share.

The Psalmist says that compassion is a characteristic of God's nature. "The Lord is gracious and full of compassion, slow to anger and of great kindness. The Lord is loving to everyone, and his compassion is over all his works." (Psalm 145:8-9)

We know that Jesus had a compassionate heart. He fed the hungry and showed mercy to those who were sick, troubled, or grieved because of their separation from God. His first response to people in trouble was not to condemn but to enter into their suffering to relieve pain and to give them hope. He invited the weary and those with heavy burdens to rest in him. As he said, "I am gentle and humble in heart, and you will find rest for your souls. For my yoke is easy, and my burden is light." (Matt. 11:28-30)

I can't imagine any of us disagreeing with this endeavor to live compassionate lives. We do this in our church life and in personal responses to natural disasters and tragedies near and throughout the world. But being compassionate is not always easy. One can become so distressed by seeing the suffering of others that one turns a blind eye. We might think, "If I don't see it, it won't bother me – and perhaps it will go away on its own." It is particularly difficult to show compassion to those whose suffering is self-inflicted. We are likely to blame the victim. If, for example, one were not addicted to drugs, alcohol, sex, or crime, one wouldn't need to suffer the consequences of those poor choices. That attitude, of course, holds some truth. We often put ourselves into the predicaments from which we suffer. Sometimes we do this willfully, and at other times it is the result of our ignorance. Most of us don't intend to be bad people. We were created as good people, but in our weakness and lack of wisdom we do destructive things.

The question then becomes, "Is it enough to condemn bad behavior and the person who does it? Is it enough to condemn those who are poor because they haven't found jobs? Is it enough to maintain prejudices because our stereotypes of other races may on occasion be true? Do I, for example, need to care for the cancer patient who smoked cigarettes for years? Don't people with AIDS deserve what they got?"

It is not enough to blame the victim. If that were the proper response, God would not have gone to the trouble to express compassion for us in the person of Jesus, even to death on a cross for the sake of love. God in Christ knows our weakness and would rather suffer with us than discard us. We are precious to God even when we don't know what we are doing.

An alternative to compassion is to point the finger at those who fail because of poor choices or who live in ways contrary to one's own values. In conflict situations in particular we tend to get satisfaction rallying people around us who agree with us. It makes us feel as if we are right and the others wrong. The problem with this kind of thinking is that we become "absorbed with our own self-image" and fail to empathize with others. Being right replaces being loving. Whether we are right or wrong, this kind of thinking can be dangerous because it hardens our hearts.

Compassion is not concerned with protecting one's self-image. It is the ability to act with selfless love responding spontaneously to the needs of others. It is not a matter of being right. Jesus didn't require holiness before he acted. In fact he said that the prostitutes, tax collectors, and sinners would enter the kingdom of God before those who patted themselves on the back for offering pious prayers in the temple. One did not have to sign a statement of orthodoxy or recite a creed before receiving the gift of healing. To be made whole one simply needed to put one's trust in God's mercy and forgiveness. Love happens in relationship, not in a dogmatism that rejects or ignores the suffering of others.

Our challenge is to learn to embrace rather than to strike back – "to be slow to anger and of great kindness."

Give us compassionate hearts, O God, that we may love you in all persons and in all things. Help us to act and speak only out of your love, and leave the judging to your mercy.

From a Fault to a Hug

We've all had experience saying and doing things that we wish we hadn't said or done. It could have been at a moment of anger when we struck back at someone who annoyed us. It might have been a simple slip of the tongue intended for humor that wasn't funny. Most days go by with a reminder that we're not perfect. We make mistakes that hurt us and offend others. Left alone the offense becomes a burden. Forgiveness seems to be the only source for relief. "I'm sorry" and "You're forgiven" are welcome words we need to hear in order to move forward in positive, loving ways.

Personal imperfections are handled in a variety of ways. If we've broken a law and get caught there are likely to be consequences – a fine or jail time. If the indiscretion is not subject to the law, it is probably about a personal issue between people. No punishment is inflicted except for the pain one feels being hurt or having hurt someone else. If the flaw is perceived as an act against God, it may be in prayer that one seeks forgiveness and a renewed chance to live a holy life.

In the spiritual life many of the saints experienced such deep regret for their failures that they inflicted punishment upon themselves. Since God didn't strike them with a bolt of lightning they took matters into their own hands. Some practiced their penance to extremes. The cross became an example of the suffering of Jesus that should be emulated. Suffering in these practices becomes a devotional, thought to be pleasing to God.

St. Rose of Lima (1586-1617), for example, in penance and in remembrance of Christ's crown of thorns, wore on her head a circlet of silver studded with sharp pricks. Others have worn hair shirts or flagellated themselves with leather straps, or starved themselves to near death. They seemed to think that for mercy God requires punishment, an idea carried over from our Jewish heritage of animal sacrifices burnt to appease God's wrath.

While these extreme practices of penance may have been offered with good intentions, they miss the point. Jesus taught that God is not trying to get even with us. Rather, God loves the sinner and wants to restore us to life. The Good Shepherd doesn't spank the lost sheep for running away. Instead, he takes the lost sheep "and lays it on his shoulders and rejoices" that the lost has been found. (Luke 15:3-7)

Nan Merrill in her *Psalms for Praying* captures the essence of the psalms and expresses them in the light of God's love and mercy. In Psalm 51 her paraphrase shows that God desires to teach us to know our weaknesses and the shortcomings that bind us, and to know the unloving ways that separate us from recognizing God's presence in our lives. In spite of our failures, we come to understand that we were brought forth in love. Love is our birthright. We then pray for forgiveness for all that binds us in fear, that we may be free to radiate love. "Cleanse me that your light might shine in me. Fill me with gladness; help me to transform weakness into strength. Look not on my past mistakes but on the aspirations of my heart. Create in me a clean heart, O Gracious One, and put a new and right spirit within me."

Prayer of this kind helps us to get back on track when we harm ourselves or someone else. Saying I'm sorry with resulting forgiveness is not meant to be a miserable process. Unfortunately, the problem is sometimes in our ability to forgive ourselves. God might be able to forgive us but we think we deserve punishment. Wallowing in this misery, however, turns us into victims – an unhealthy and prideful condition. "Beat me up, Lord" is a misguided prayer that denies the generosity of God's love and mercy.

If you have foibles needing forgiveness, turn as quickly as you can to ask for forgiveness and receive it, and move on with a right sense of yourself in God's eyes. The Good Shepherd isn't out to "get us." He wants to give each one of us a hug.

Gentleness

With media shocking us daily announcing worldwide violence, it seems good to take a moment to think about gentleness. Gentleness by contrast is a warm and courteous trait that reminds us of gentle men and gentle women. It may also carry a social attribute of refinement expected in upper class southern society. But this gentleness doesn't mean that one is weak. Gentle people often respond to conflict quietly and with patience. Even those who don't have a naturally gentle temperament can learn to keep their inner turmoil under control. Gandhi and Martin Luther King were forceful leaders who didn't always appear as saints, but they advocated kindness rather than drafting legions to fight. Their gentleness came from strong wills committed to peace. They didn't add fuel to fires seeking revenge for their opposition. It took strength to remain gentle.

In his letter to the Galatians, Paul gave a list of behaviors to avoid, and by contrast the fruits of the Spirit. Qualities to emulate are "love, joy, peace, patience, kindness, generosity, faithfulness, gentleness, and self-control." It probably takes several of these gifts to live any one. Gentleness, for example, seems to require kindness. The gentle people I know are kind, giving them an aura of love and peace. Perhaps all the fruits of the Spirit are meant to be absorbed to bring harmony to relationships.

James Kavanaugh, a former Roman Catholic priest, poet, and writer referred in poetry and other writings that "there are men too gentle to live among wolves." He described himself as a searcher who continued to explore life, hoping to uncover its ultimate secret. He wrote, "We searchers are ambitious only for life itself, for everything beautiful it can provide. Most of all we love and want to be loved. We want to live in a relationship that will not impede our wandering, nor prevent our search, nor lock us in prison walls; that will take us for what little we have to give. We do not want to prove ourselves to another or compete for love. For wanderers, dreamers, and lovers, for lonely men and women who dare to ask of life everything good and beautiful. It is for those who are too gentle to live among wolves."

In his poem by this title he describes the difficulty gentle people have trying to be searchers in a world where those with greedy claws prepare their victims for burial.

There are men too gentle to live among wolves
Who prey upon them with IBM eyes
And sell their hearts and guts for martinis at noon.
There are men too gentle for a savage world
Who dream instead of snow and children and Halloween
And wonder if the leaves will change their color soon.

There are men too gentle to live among wolves
Who anoint them for burial with greedy claws
And murder them for a merchant's profit and gain.
There are men too gentle for a corporate world
Who dream instead of candied apples and Ferris wheels
And pause to hear the distant whistle of a train.

There are men too gentle to live among wolves
Who devour them with eager appetite and search
For other men to prey upon and suck their childhood dry.
There are men too gentle for an accountant's world
Who dream instead of Easter eggs and fragrant grass
And search for beauty in the mystery of the sky.

There are men too gentle to live among wolves
Who toss them like a lost and wounded dove.
Such gentle men are lonely in a merchant's world,
Unless they have a gentle one to love.

Kavanaugh beautifully describes the difficulty gentle people have in a world that often coerces us into the kingdom of profit and gain, and sucks dry the memory of childhood. Such flags present a challenge to pursue – a willingness to continue our search for real values that honor the goodness of the Spirit's fruits. Accepting this mission requires self-control – a refusal to join the pack; and in our fears, not to respond with rotten fruit: with "enmities, strife, jealousy, anger, quarrels, dissensions, factions, envy…and things like these." Hopefully, we will not surrender to the tactics of wolves attempting to thwart their bitter bite with bigger jaws. The end seldom justifies the means.

Strength in our weakness is the discipline that can bring us the joys of love and peace; and through kindness and gentleness to learn patience, generosity, faithfulness, and self-control. In what may seem a lonely journey, may we each have a gentle one to love.

September 11th Anniversary

(Published September 9, 2011)

This weekend is the tenth anniversary of the September 11, 2001, terrorist attacks when almost 3,000 people perished after hijacked planes slammed into the World Trade Center in New York City, the Pentagon in Washington, D.C., and a field in Shanksville, Pennsylvania.

The pain and anger resulting from these events is still being felt. As the Presiding Bishop of the Episcopal Church, Katharine Jefferts Schori said, "Many people died senselessly that day, and many still grieve their loss…but this anniversary is an opportunity for reflection, to work for healing and reconciliation. We believe there is hope."

Some acts of violence seem unforgivable. Our immediate reaction to these attacks is to repay evil with evil, "an eye for an eye." But we know that process leads to everyone becoming blind.

While these acts of terror were planned and created to be heroic, we experienced them as evil. Similar violence occurs on a daily basis throughout the world. Such terror is a far cry from Jesus' admonition to "Love your enemies, and pray for those who persecute you." (Matt. 5:43-45)

In our everyday lives we seldom deal with issues this grave. People do hurt us, however, sometimes intentionally and at other times not knowing what they have done. They live in what my father called, "invincible ignorance." They don't know themselves; they don't value relationships; or they are so consumed with a need to maintain power that they refuse to humble themselves to the point where they will admit wrongdoing. This is common, and it is regrettable.

On this tenth anniversary of the 09/11 terrorist attacks on our country, this point hits home in a painful way. But whether it is terrorists or an individual's failure to admit guilt should not lock us into anger for a lifetime. We do not give up hope for healing and reconciliation.

Here is a prayer to help us remember our loss and look to the future with hope:

God of steadfast love, who led your people through the wilderness: Be with us as we remember and grieve our losses on this anniversary of September 11, 2001. By your grace, bring us healing, and lead us in the path of new life and peace, in the company of your saints and angels; through Jesus Christ, the Savior and Redeemer of the world. Amen.

The Earth Is the Lord's

The Psalmist sings, "The earth is the Lord's and all that is in it, the world and all who dwell therein." (Psalm 24:1)

From ancient times people have understood that God is the creator of the universe and that it is sacred because it belongs to God. People of faith understand this, and most recognize the sacred responsibility we have to care for the creation God has given us as our earthly home.

Yet, there are too many examples demonstrating how we have squandered our inheritance by not making a right use of the gifts of creation. Pollution and global warming confront us repeatedly. Even from the early days of our nation, settlers moved into new territories, used up the land and wildlife, and then moved on to greener pastures. Perhaps the country seemed too big to mar with seeming little indiscretions.

Native Americans, however, realized the problem when the first settlers took over their lands. While Christians received the Jewish understanding of the earth being the Lord's, Native Americans reverenced the sacredness of the earth in a much deeper sense. The whites considered the land something to be bought and sold. As Seattle, chief of the Suquamish (1786?-1866) observed, "How can you buy and sell the sky, the warmth of the land? The idea is strange to us...Every part of this earth is sacred to my people. Every shining pine needle, every sandy shore, every mist in the dark woods, every clearing and humming insect is holy in the memory and experience of my people...We are part of the earth and it is part of us."

Seattle who became a Christian cooperated peacefully with the federal government to obtain the best of what he thought possible to prevent the extinction of his people. In 1855 Seattle signed the Port Elliott Treaty, which transferred ancestral Indian lands to the federal government and established a reservation for Native American tribes in the Northwest region. But he took the opportunity in a letter to

President Franklin Pierce to express his profound ecological concerns and spiritual vision.

"We know that the White Man does not understand our ways. One portion of the land is the same to him as the next, for he is a stranger who comes in the night and takes from the land whatever he needs. The earth is not his brother, but his enemy, and when he has conquered it, he moves on."

"One thing we know, which the White Man may one day discover – our God is the same God. You may think now that you own Him as you wish to own our land; but you cannot. He is the God of humanity, and his compassion is equal for the red man and the white. The earth is precious to him, and to harm the earth is to heap contempt on its Creator…Even the white man cannot be exempt from the common destiny. We may be brothers after all. We shall see." (See *All Saints*, R. Ellsberg)

One would hope that we in the 21ˢᵗ century would reflect on this haunting and prophetic document conveyed in the 19ᵗʰ century. It is time to respond to Chief Seattle's message with right action, not only to preserve the earth and its creatures, but to honor the God to whom it all belongs.

Tick…Tock, Tick…Tock

Tick…tock, tick…tock, speaks the clock. In my home there are thirty-three clocks – some that speak, others dormant due to long use, and those living by electric power. What they have in common is an ability to tell that time marches on…with or without my awareness or permission.

As we grow in age we begin to reflect on our past lives and wonder what the future holds. Most people nearing retirement make plans so they will be prepared financially and be surrounded by family and friends. For those who have reached this age the time may seem to have come suddenly as if overnight. The clock kept ticking even when we didn't take notice.

In our spiritual lives it is important to live each moment as it arrives. As is often said, God is present in the "now" of our lives. We don't have to wait to begin to live fulfilling lives. God is present as the clock ticks as we move through the rhythm of each day. Each moment can become an encounter with God.

J. Philip Newell says it beautifully in a morning prayer:
Early in the morning I seek your presence, O God,
not because you are ever absent from me
but because often I am absent from you
at the heart of each moment where you forever dwell.
In the rising of the sun,
in the unfolding color and shape of the morning
open my eyes to the mystery of this moment
that in every moment of the day
I may know your life-giving presence.
Open my eyes to this moment that in every moment
I may know you as the One who is always now.

The ticking of the clock need not mark lost time but time lived to the fullest in the present moment. Enjoy the One who is never absent from us but who is always present in the "now" of our lives.

Take Time to Notice

Mark Nepo in his book, *The Book of Awakening,* tells a story about himself becoming a slave to a schedule he created. He writes, "I wake clear and rested, light flooding my room. The day seems endless and free. But making coffee, I notice three bills I haven't paid, and after showering, I notice I need a haircut, and since I'll be out that way, I think I might as well pick up my shirts. But I so want to spend time in the sun. So I think, well, after these errands, I'll go to the park, and then I deliberate which park will be just right and decide on one forty minutes away." He continues to add to his schedule until he is interrupted by a small bird. He lifts his head to see the chirping bird just as a cloud opens and the light floods his mind, at which point he drops all his plans "like change on the ground." Having taken notice of what he was doing to himself, he began to laugh.

I imagine that many of us could tell a similar story. We keep ourselves busy as if our worth depended on what we do rather than who we are. We keep our nose to the grindstone forgetting that our true worth comes from the way God sees us – as good. We don't have to earn God's love for us. God's love is a gift. And even the one with the fewest merit badges is equal to the one with the most.

If we don't believe this, and get into a rut of perpetual "doing," we are likely to miss a lot in life that didn't appear on our agendas. As a reminder to take time to notice God's presence in all of life, I say with my prayers a line from the movie, "The Color Purple." With a slight paraphrase the line goes: "God gets upset when you don't notice the color purple." In the past I have missed the beauty of wildflowers, conversations that didn't have my full attention because I was thinking about the next thing I needed to accomplish, and time lost with my family because I was doing something for them instead of being with them.

Being a slave to the schedules we create can affect our spiritual lives too when we get so busy doing things for God that we don't take time to be present for God – in creation, in the Christ spirit that lives in others, in the silence. A little listening and a look up and around might become an antidote for the compulsive schedules that keep us from living a full life.

Take time to notice. God is in the present moment. Don't miss it.

The Gospel of Bad News

The word "gospel" means good news, yet we frequently hear the message of Christianity portrayed as bad news. Instead of recalling Jesus' ministry of healing and hope, care for the poor and outcasts, and God's ultimate nature as Love, we hear that most people who have ever lived are going to hell because they haven't been baptized or professed their faith as required by some denomination or group of people. A message that is meant to be good news becomes bad news. It is no wonder that an increasing number of young adults who hear this bad news are leaving the church and are searching for spiritual meaning for their lives outside traditional Christian structures. This negative god is nothing more than an idol.

Edward Hays has pointed out that the most popular idol today is not made of silver or gold but, paradoxically, is a deformed god! This idol is made by stripping away all the mystery from the Divine One to create a small, understandable God in order to explain whatever we find unexplainable. He has noted that among the false gods there is a "sin-punishing God; or a 'you-had-it coming', retaliating God. Institutions easily make idols out of themselves that require unquestioned loyalty, obedience, and sacrifice." (*A Book of Wonders*)

Regrettably, as an old adage says, "All idols require human sacrifices." The sacrifices are not the result of faithful people living out a commitment of compassion and service, even to risking their lives, but to being sacrificed by those who alone consider themselves worthy of heaven. Those on the altars of sacrifice are often people dealing with relational and moral struggles, the poor who cannot afford to satisfy a conservative political agenda, and those whose sexual orientation is lesbian, gay, bisexual, or transgender. Such people are often not viewed as children created in the image and likeness of God, but as the condemned. A message of fear to alarm the public is, "Don't go to hell with them." This idol god replaces the God of Wonder, Love, Forgiveness, Mercy and Reconciliation.

If you find yourself worshipping a fake god, avoid becoming a human sacrifice to that idol.

When Scripture Contradicts Itself

It has been said that one can prove almost anything with a line from Scripture. This assumes that the line you pick is inerrant truth. But trouble arrives when two passages are picked that contradict each other. For example, in the Hebrew Scriptures we read that proper punishment for a crime deserves retribution in like manner. "Anyone who kills a human being shall be put to death. Anyone who kills an animal shall make restitution for it, life for life. Anyone who maims another shall suffer the same injury in return: fracture for fracture, eye for eye, tooth for tooth; the injury inflicted is the injury to be suffered." (Lev. 24:17-20) This law from Leviticus is still used to support capital punishment. "Anyone who kills a human being shall be put to death." That's what the Bible says.

By contrast, those who oppose capital punishment are likely to quote Jesus who said, "You have heard that it was said, 'An eye for an eye and a tooth for a tooth.' But I say to you, do not resist an evildoer. But if one strikes you on the right cheek, turn the other also." Later in this teaching Jesus says, "You have heard that it was said, 'You shall love your neighbor and hate your enemy.' But I say to you, love your enemies and pray for those who persecute you.'" (Matt. 5:38-45) One's intended proof of conduct from Scripture can be seen from opposite perspectives.

In the Second Letter to the Thessalonians (3:10-12) there is an issue regarding work which could be easily quoted by conservatives. "Anyone unwilling to work should not eat. For we hear that some of you are living in idleness, mere busybodies, not doing any work. Now such persons we command and exhort in the Lord Jesus Christ to do their work quietly and to earn their own living."

Most people would probably agree with this assessment. Those who work are not in favor of allowing people who are able to work to just sit at home by their widescreen TV's waiting for the arrival of food stamps, free health care, a disability check, and early retirement benefits. As referenced, if you don't work you don't eat. This may be the proper response in this scenario. But Jesus always advocated that the poor be fed. We don't read of a condition that would justify leaving a person to starve to death.

Another way of looking at this issue is likely to come from liberal minded people who advocate social relief programs to aid those who are not able to work or care for themselves. A passage from Matthew's Gospel might be referred to as told by Jesus who imagines the last judgment with the king sitting on his throne. The king will say to some, "Come, you that are blessed by my Father, inherit the kingdom prepared for you from the foundation of the world; for I was hungry and you gave me food, I was thirsty and you gave me something to drink, I was a stranger and you welcomed me, I was naked and you gave me clothing, I was sick and you took care of me, I was in prison and you visited me." Then the righteous will ask Jesus when he needed any of this care that they overlooked. After a full explanation Jesus says, "Truly I tell you, just as you did not do it to one of the least of these, you did not do it to me." (Matt. 25: 31-46)

The Scripture gives us at least two ways to view a proper response to human need. We have seen that advocates taking seemingly opposite points of view managed to shut down the federal government for 16 days in 2013 arguing about how to deal with these issues. Do you fund social programs to satisfy human need, or instead of giving a person a fish to eat you teach that person how to fish?

While the reader can determine a solution, it is appropriate to recognize current events as they might have been addressed at another time in Scripture. How we apply what we read to problems today will vary; and from observed divisions in government, opposing parties can become immobilized in polarized camps. "My way or the highway" may work for despots, but that's not the way to arrive at a mutual understanding that will allow people to respect one another even with differing views. We can continue to be adamant about causes that we believe enhance the private and public good; but somewhere in that enthusiasm one needs to be watchful not to abuse others when programs become more important than persons. In the extreme, fanatical fervor leads to witch hunts, inquisitions, and genocide.

When we use the Bible as a resource for determining personal conduct and the welfare of the community, we might begin by praying a prayer Episcopalians say: "Blessed Lord, who has caused all holy Scriptures to be written for our learning; Grant us so to hear them, read, mark, learn, and inwardly digest them, that we may embrace and ever hold fast the blessed hope of everlasting life, which you have given us in our Savior Jesus Christ; who lives and reigns with you and the Holy Spirit, one God, for ever and ever. Amen."

Bible Stories

The Bible is filled with stories. Some were written to recall the heritage and traditions of the Hebrew people, such as the story of Moses and the Ten Commandments. In the New Testament there are accounts of Jesus' life and of early Christians. These stories are a mixture of history and story telling to express the faith of early Christians. Scholars continue to use linguistic, literal-allegorical, historical-critical, and archaeological methods to establish any historical realities behind the texts.

The Bible also contains myths that were created to explain a truth without having any historic or scientific merit. Stories in this category are the two creation myths in the Book of Genesis that give God credit for being the creator of the universe and to recognize that even though God's creation is good there is sin in the world. These mythological stories are not meant to be taken literally just as one wouldn't take the characters in the Cinderella story as historic people. Fiction and myth often tell a truth with made up characters and events.

In the Book of Genesis, for example, the theological intent is to say that the world and Israel belong to God. The opening story of creation is not a scientific treatise verifying that the universe was created in six twenty-four hour periods (astronomers noting that the universe is 13.7 billion years old and still evolving), but rather that life exists because of God's intent that it be so.

We learn the origins of human beings from paleo-anthropologists, not from Bible stories. Our first ancestors in this chain of evolution were homo habilis who lived about 2.5 million years ago; then homo erectus who could stand up like us 1.8 million years ago, with continuing changes down to homo sapiens to which modern humans belong. At no point was there a single first man named Adam and woman named Eve. They are just part of a story to give God credit as the creator of life even if it took God millions of years to get us where we are now.

One should not fret that all the stories in the Bible are not literally true. They were never intended to be. There are a variety of literary ways to express how people have experienced God in their lives. In fact, the idea of God changes in the Bible from early writings and experiences to those of first century Christians. The stories in themselves are not meant to give us certitude, but rather to open us up to the wonder of God, the miracle of life, and to leave us in a state of awe. Our faith is not in a book (an idol), but in the experience of the Spirit's presence in our daily lives. This varies from person to person, but we share God's identity together as sisters and brothers in a glorious creation.

Not Quite Satisfied

There are always those who are not quite satisfied with their lot in life. It may be that they missed opportunities for education and advancement as young adults. Personal and family relationships may be disappointing – a bad marriage or children struggling to find themselves. Discontent may also be caused by setting standards that are too high – a perfectionist mentality that guarantees failure.

Some people are not quite satisfied with their lot in life no matter what happens. If they accomplish a goal, there's still something missing which keeps them from being happy. The long awaited new home is not big enough, or the five-figure salary needs another zero. It's not issues of trauma that affect them. They simply have adopted a "sad sack" mentality.

Acquiring the ingredients for a satisfying life is not always easy. Beyond having the necessities of life we desire quality living that will give our lives purpose and meaning. Our minds and spirits want to be satisfied as well as our bodies.

Business, religion, and psychology know that we have these needs, and they are quick to give us answers to our dilemma of being alive but not quite satisfied. Commercials tell us that if we buy their products we will be happy. Television evangelists proclaim that if we accept their brand of religion and send money, our spiritual lives will be satisfied too. Popular psychology and self-help books tell us how to make a marriage, how to survive a divorce, and how to resolve conflicts. There is no limit to available advice for those who find their lot in life not quite satisfying.

So why is the problem so prevalent?

The temptation for any preacher is to give yet another quick fix. "Believe on the Lord Jesus Christ," some will say, and you will be saved and satisfied. No doubt there are those for whom this is true.

But hasty quick fixes don't always work. People's problems differ and cheap solutions only malign the worth of the person. Rather, we need to recognize that we are works in progress. We're like statues that don't have all the rough edges chipped away. Our shapes are often awkward and even ugly. The final product has yet to be turned into the perfect image and likeness of God.

While solutions for our discontent may take time, a place to start is to deal with our attitudes and expectations. The half full glass as we know can be seen as half full or half empty.

One can either be thankful that the glass is at least half full or be dissatisfied that it is half empty.

At the risk of reiterating the obvious, more joy is to found living our lives in the spirit of thanksgiving than perpetually focusing on our dissatisfactions. Jesus' way of expressing this was to say that we should not become anxious about our lives – what we will eat, or drink, or wear. "Is not life more than food, and the body more than clothing?" (Matt. 6:25-34) God knows our needs, and provisions are available within creation to feed and clothe us. Jesus said, however, that material goods will not in themselves give us the satisfaction we desire. Rather, our first priority should be a venture into God's kingdom and righteousness. That is where we can live beyond disappointments and find wholeness and peace.

Our lives are lived on at least two levels. One involves our participation in the purely secular world with its values and demands. That is the givenness of our lives; and we are meant to be responsible to one another in the everydayness of life. But there is another level that we can enter that will give the first level more purpose and meaning. That is the deeper level of prayer, which attends to the Spirit dwelling in us. It is a place where we are able to live beyond the superficial aspects of life and enter into an adoration of our Creator. It is a place where, if we take the time, we can be nourished with food for the soul.

Seeking the kingdom of God first will lift us out of self-pity and give us compassionate hearts. As we release selfish attachments, ambitions, and "insatiable self-pride," we will gain the freedom to minister to those outside ourselves. Rather than fretting and being anxious about our own needs, wants, and limitations, we can go forward content to live "adequate lives" that look for opportunities to express God's love and healing grace.

One of the requirements for getting part of our lives right is having the humility to know that we aren't always going to get it right. We are works in progress, and in God's time we will be made whole.

At Thanksgiving let us be grateful for all the good gifts we have received – for "the splendor of creation; for the blessing of family and friends; for tasks which demand our best efforts; for those disappointments and failures that lead us to acknowledge our dependence on God alone." And let us give thanks for our Lord Jesus Christ, who lifts us from our dissatisfaction to resurrected living.

SOURCES

Borg, Marcus, 2001: *Reading the Bible Again for the First Time: Taking the Bible Seriously But Not Literally*

Butcher, Carmen Acevedo, 2009: *The Cloud of Unknowing*

Butcher, John Beverley, 2011: *Sacred Partnership: Jesus and Mary Magdalene*

Chittister, Joan, 2008: *The Gift of Years: Growing Older Gracefully*

Countryman, L. William, 1994: *Biblical Authority or Biblical Tyranny*

di Mello, Anthony, 1990: *Taking Flight: A Book of Story Meditations*

Ellsberg, Robert, 1987: *All Saints: Daily Reflections on Saints, Prophets, and Witnesses for Our Time*

Fiand, Barbara, 2002: *In the Stillness You Will Know: Exploring the Paths of Our Ancient Belonging*

Fox, Matthew, 1983: *Meditations with Meister Eckhart*

Fulghum, Robert, 1986: *All I Really Need to Know I Learned in Kindergarten*

Hays, Edward, 2009: *A Book of Wonders: Daily Reflections for Awakened Living*

Henry, O (William Sydney Porter), 1905: *The Gift of the Magi*

Kavanaugh, James, 1970: *There Are Men Too Gentle to Live Among Wolves*

Keating, Thomas, 1992: *Open Mind, Open Heart*

Ladinsky, Daniel, 2002: *Love Poems from God: Twelve Sacred Voices from the East and West*

Manchester, William, 1992: *A World Lit Only By Fire: The Medieval Mind and the Renaissance: Portrait of an Age*

Merrill, Nan, 2007: *Psalms for Praying: An Invitation to Wholeness*

Merton, Thomas, 1961: *New Seeds of Contemplation*

Merton, Thomas, 1956: *Thoughts in Solitude*

Mother Teresa, 1997: *In the Heart of the World: Thoughts, Stories, and Prayers*

Nepo, Mark, 2000: *The Book of Awakening: Having the Life You Want by Being Present to the Life You Have*

Newell, J. Philip, 2002: *Sounds of the Eternal: A Celtic Psalter*

Oliver, Mary, 2011: *A Year's Risings and Four Sonnets*

Oliver, Mary, 2008: *Red Bird*

Rohr, Richard, 1999: *Everything Belongs: The Gift of Contemplative Prayer*

Singh, Kathleen D., 1998: *The Grace in Dying: A Message of Hope, Comfort and Spiritual Transformation*

St. John of the Cross, 1979: *Collected Works*

St. John of the Cross, 1972: *The Poems*

St. Teresa of Avila, 1980: *The Collected Works*

Wiesel, Elie, 1979: *The Trial of God*

Wiman, Christian, 2013: *My Bright Abyss: Meditation of a Modern Believer*

Made in the USA
Lexington, KY
30 November 2014